REFORMATION, REVOLUTION

AND

REBIRTH

The Story of the Return of Catholicism to Reading
and the
Founding of St James' Parish

John Mullaney and Lindsay Mullaney

Scallop Shell Press

ISBN 978-0-9572772-0-5

Published by Scallop Shell Press

29 Derby Road,
Caversham
Reading
RG4 5HE

FOREWORD
by
CANON JOHN O'SHEA, PARISH PRIEST

In 2010 I arrived in Reading knowing only a little of the history of St James' Church and it has been my privilege to become part of a community with a very rich heritage.

In December 2012 the parish community of St James' will celebrate the 175th anniversary of the laying of the foundation stone of the Church. This significant anniversary has initiated a major refurbishment of the Church of St James and the production of this publication. Perhaps it is also worth noting that this is the 200th anniversary of the consecration of the Chapel of the Resurrection here in Reading which preceded the Church of St James. At this time we also celebrate the 50th anniversary of the opening of the Second Vatican Council, an event which transformed the life of the Church and inspired it to engage with the developments of today's world. This vision has been the guiding light for my life as a priest over the past forty years

Anniversaries always call for a celebration, a time to reflect and a time to honour the memory of those who have gone before us. They provide us with the opportunity to give thanks to God for their lives of faith, their memory, and their fidelity to the Catholic way of life. This has been passed on from generation to generation.

This is a story that needs to be told, needs to be recorded and handed on to the next generation.

St James' Church is built on holy ground, it is the place where the monks of Reading Abbey prayed and celebrated the sacred liturgy together in word and song. The last Abbot, Hugh Cook Faringdon, was martyred for the faith just a short distance from where St James' Church now stands.

The story of the growth of the Catholic faith in Reading is due in no small way to the arrival of the French priests and I want to pay particular tribute to the memory of François Longuet who is buried in the crypt at St James Church. He made a significant contribution to the wider community in Reading, sadly he was murdered on his way back to Reading along the Oxford Road.

Finally, I wish to thank John and Lindsay Mullaney for their efforts to research this publication. It has taken them to many different libraries here in England and in France. We owe them an immense debt of gratitude for ensuring that the story of the growth of the Catholic faith in Reading has been kept alive. I would also like to pay tribute to the Archives-Heritage group attached to St James as they too have contributed to this publication.

BACKGROUND

Some thirty years ago I was asked by Canon Edward Conway to write a history of St James' Church and School. After much research, a small booklet giving an overview of the founding of the Parish was produced. It contained only a fraction of the material that had been unearthed. A few years later, after Canon Conway had left the Parish, additions were made to bring the booklet up to date. For over a quarter of a century this served as the only record in print of the fascinating story of how St. James' came to be founded and why the Church was built in the midst of Reading's most historic site, the Abbey Ruins.

In 2011 Canon John O'Shea formed an Archive group and asked if I would like to join. Its purpose was to catalogue the documents held in the Parish. This proved painstaking work and I was pleased to discover that so much had been preserved. Unfortunately, since I undertook my original research, some material has inevitably been lost or dissipated.

Under the chairmanship of Canon O'Shea, the Archive Group soon extended its role. It organised the erection of a plaque to Blessed Dominic Barberi on the site of his death. It was involved in welcoming and organising a visit from the Confraternity of St James and, for the first time in its history, St James' Parish took part in the annual Heritage Day events during which over 400 people visited the Church.

By one of those serendipitous quirks of timing, David Cliffe of Reading Libraries was in the process of planning a day's conference with the theme *Catholic Reading*. He asked specialist speakers to talk about three periods covering the history of Catholicism in Reading, starting with the Middle Ages and the founding of the Abbey, through the years of persecution and recusancy and finishing with a talk about how and why Catholicism returned to Reading in the late 18th century and early 19th century. He asked if I could cover this last period.

Since much of this part of the research involved the arrival of French clergy during the Revolutionary period, it made sense to ask my wife, Lindsay, a fluent French speaker, to come onto the team. As such Lindsay has concentrated on the French aspect of our researches. Many of the documents, even those written by Englishmen, such as Bishop Poynter, in the first quarter of the 19th century, are in French. Many of these English priests had begun their studies at the English College in Douai, France and it is clear that their influence was very strong in the formation of the emerging Catholic congregation at the time.

And so our researches have taken us from Reading Library, a five-minute walk from the Church, to the Diocesan Archives of Westminster and Portsmouth and as far afield as Normandy, where not only did Reading's great medieval Abbey have its roots 900 years ago but from where the founding fathers of St James' parish came as refugees 700 years later.

John Mullaney 2012

PREFACE

Our purpose is to present the reader with an informative and readable overview of how the Church of St. James came into existence. Our researches have been subjected to rigorous historical methodology but we hope their presentation is accessible to all. For this reason we have not included too many references to our sources. Where we have had to rely on secondary material we have made every attempt to seek out primary validating evidence. This has been achieved mainly by referring to contemporary correspondence and records held in several archives. We have sought corroboration from newspaper reports, maps and local directories of the time.

The research is ongoing and, at the time of writing, there are several intriguing problems which we are pursuing and to which at the present we do not know the answers. We have tried not to make unjustified assumptions. But part of the fun of history is to propose possible and likely scenarios based on existing evidence, only to come across something which casts new light on the issue.

We hope you will be intrigued by our story and stimulated to find out more for yourselves.

John and Lindsay Mullaney

ACKNOWLEDGEMENTS

First of all our thanks go to Tony Tinkel and John Radice for undertaking the task of proof reading our manuscript, spotting errors and making valuable suggestions.

In addition we should like to thank the following individuals and organisations who have helped in our researches:

Eric and Helen Stanford; David Cliffe; David and Mary Langford; Sidney Gold; Westmister Diocesan Archives; Dr Val Fontana and Portsmouth Diocesan Archives; Reading Library; Reading Museum; The National Portrait Gallery; Elizabeth Einberg; Mary Beale; John R Mullaney; James Mullaney; Anne Carey; Jack Eyston and Lady Anne of Mapledurham House; The Hon. Georgina Stonor; Philippa Hunter; Pembroke College, Cambridge; St Edmund's College, Ware; Winchester Catholic Archives; John Radice; and members of the Archive Group, St James', Reading.

Most of all we should like to thank Canon John O'Shea for initiating this research project and for all his encouragement and support.

CONTENTS

SECTION A

REFORMATION AND REVOLUTION

PART 1

The National and International Background to the Return of Catholicism to Reading

PART 2

The Return of Catholicism to Reading, 1790 – 1817

PART 3

SAINT JAMES' CHURCH

The Wheble Family and the Building of St. James' Church: The Wheble Family – Abbé Pierre Louis Guy Miard de la Blardière – The Abbey Ruins and James Wheble – The First 'Parish Priest' of St James' Church.

Pugin's First Church Design - The Building and Opening of St James' Church: Laying the Foundation Stone, 1837 – Pugin and the Norman Romanesque Style – The Official Opening of St James', 1840.

PART 4

PUGIN AND THE DESIGN OF THE CHURCH

The Question about the Original Design: The Abbey Ruins – The Norman-Romanesque Style.

The True Principles **and their Application to St James' Church**: The Principles of Architecture – Columns and Buttresses – The West Front – Pinnacles – The Roof – Gables – The East End – Mouldings – Mouldings and the West Door – The Windows – The Metalwork – The Woodwork – Conclusion.

The Abbey Ruins and the Forbury after 1841.

The Abbey Ruins and Reading Today.

APPENDICES **Page 149**

A. Letter to the English People: A poem by N. Leguay, a French Priest.

B. Obituary of Anna Maria Smart

C. Catalogue of Longuet's Books at the House in Vastern Lane.

D. The Consecration of St. James' Church at Reading, The Tablet, August 1840.

E. Pugin's Letter to Father Ringrose, August 1840

.

F. St James' Archive Group.

BIBLIOGRAPHY AND SOURCES **Page 156**

THE AUTHORS AND OTHER CONTRIBUTORS **Page 158**

SECTION A

REFORMATION
AND
REVOLUTION

PART 1

The National and International Background

to the

Return of Catholicism to Reading

CHAPTER 1

Historical Background

Introduction

The fifty or so years from 1790 to 1840 saw a revolution in the status of Catholicism in England.

The 18th century was a time of revolution. It was the century which saw the war for American Independence. It was an era when the ideal of civic equality was redefined. It was a time when the duties, as well as the rights, of lawmakers, were codified. It was the century when the ideas of Revolutionary France, of liberty, equality and fraternity, with their all-embracing concept of 'democracy,' were spread throughout the world.

Based on the philosophies of such as Locke, Hume and Rousseau, a new vision of governance, a social contract, had been created and was evolving throughout that emerging phenomenon, the Western World. Even when the 'reality' fell far short of the 'ideal', its philosophical concepts gave the common man a new status in society. True, the roots of these movements could be traced back to the 'freedoms' of the late Middle Ages. The precept of *stadtluft macht frei* (city air brings freedom), was an early battle cry of liberty in Germanic lands. During the mid 17th century, England exploded in violent revolution culminating in regicide and Parliamentary rule. Regal Divine Right was swept away by the ideals and practice of Parliamentary Might. In the words of a contemporary ballad, the world had indeed been turned upside down.

It was also the century of a revolution in the methods of industrial and agricultural production. It was a century which saw a revolution in the arts. It was the century of the great Bach dynasty, of Handel, Mozart, Haydn and Beethoven. Constable and Turner revolutionised painting, whilst Goethe's own *harrowing of hell* stormed through, and swept away, earlier preconceptions about literature and its uses.

A new political era dawned with the emergence of nationalism and capitalism, and their concomitant counterparts of internationalism and socialism. These, and their arguably more fearful hybrids, fascism and communism, were to dominate the next century and beyond, culminating in two world wars and spawning conflicting political ideologies.

Britain's role as a trading nation, with its global territorial expansionist policies and its relationship with other world powers, was intertwined with all the above. But to

7

understand Britain's standing in the 18th century, and its relationship with other nations, it is necessary to look at an earlier clash of ideologies: one based on religion and its struggle with secular power rather than a contest between different political ideologies.

Since 1555 and the Peace of Augsburg much of Europe accepted that the solution to the problem of who held the right to govern lay within the great compromise of *cuis regio eius religio,* (the ruler's religion determines that of his people). This gave the prevailing civil authority the right to determine the religion of its subjects, a view diametrically opposed to the 'freedoms' and 'liberties' espoused by the Enlightened thinkers of the 18th century.

To a great extent the story of the return of Catholicism to England, and its practical effects on the lives of ordinary people, which we shall see in the course of this book, is the story of the conflict between these two world-views.

Catholicism, The Protestant Succession and the Religious Question

Anti-Catholic legislation in England was rooted in the question of the Protestant claim to the throne. The draconian penalties imposed on Catholics were the result of fears and suspicions dating from the 16th century and specifically from Elizabethan times.

There was a justifiable anxiety that the Church of Rome, Catholic European states such as Spain and France, and even individual Catholics in England, were plotting to oust the ruling monarch. Just to be a Catholic in England was to raise doubts about national loyalty. The question had to be asked whether just being a Catholic entailed harbouring treasonable inclinations. The Rising in the North at the time of Queen Elizabeth, the Gunpowder Plot of 1605 at the time of the Stuart, James I and the 18th century Jacobite rebellions against the Hanoverians, all served to confirm this suspicion.

And so the legislation that was enacted over the two centuries following the 1570s was designed to restrict at best, and to persecute at worst, those with 'Papist' leanings.

To understand the causes of the problem it is necessary to take a look at the *Elizabethan Settlement.*

In 1569 there was a major Catholic rising in the North. The goal was to free Mary Stuart, Queen of Scots, who after fleeing Scotland became Elizabeth's prisoner, marry her to Thomas Howard, Duke of Norfolk, and put her on the English throne. After their defeat over 750 of the rebels were executed on Elizabeth's orders.

However, in 1570, believing that the revolt had been successful, Pope Pius V issued a Bull, a Papal edict, *Regnans in Excelsis*. In this he declared *Elizabeth, the pretended Queen of England and the servant of crime* to be excommunicate and a heretic, thereby releasing her subjects from any duty of allegiance. More difficult still for English Catholics was the fact that if they obeyed Elizabeth's laws they were themselves threatened with excommunication. Not surprisingly the Bull provoked further legislation against Catholics by Parliament. The era of the Penal Laws had begun.

After 1570 missionary priests from continental seminaries came to England secretly for the *re-conversion of England* to Catholicism. In reaction, by 1581, Parliament had passed laws which made it a treasonable offence, carrying the death penalty, to convert English subjects to Catholicism with *the intent* to withdraw them from their allegiance to Elizabeth. Many priests and lay people alike were executed.

Mary Stuart continued to be the focus of Catholic dissent. From the Ridolfi Plot in 1571, when Elizabeth spared Mary but executed the Duke of Norfolk, through to the Babington Plot of 1586, it was clear that certain Catholics in England and abroad were intent on what today we would call régime change. The gulf between Catholics and Protestants was widening and the threats to the Protestant succession were not passing with the passage of time.

Two events helped buttress Elizabeth's position. One was undoubtedly the execution of Mary Stuart. This removed the immediate focal point of rebellion. The other was the failed Spanish invasion of England in 1588, with the defeat of the Spanish Armada.

It was expected by Elizabeth's opponents in continental Europe that the prospect of invasion would be a signal for English Catholics to rise in rebellion. In fact, despite the anti-Catholic laws, despite the persecutions, many, if not most, English Catholics opposed the invasion. And yet this display of patriotism did little to restore confidence by their Protestant countrymen in the loyalty of English Catholics. For the next century and a half, Catholics were marginalised.

Sentiment throughout the country moved with historical events, sometimes tolerating, sometimes actively seeking out and persecuting Catholics, but always suspicious of them. Many wealthy Catholic families survived by keeping a low profile and relying on a network of sympathetic friends and relatives within the Protestant establishment. Many others lost all they had, many fled abroad and many compromised their Faith and accepted the reformed religion.

CHAPTER 2

The Penal Laws in the Eighteenth Century

Enforcement

The Penal Laws remained in force until the late eighteenth century. However, as the century progressed and with the spread of the more liberal ideas of the Enlightenment, their enforcement was not rigorous. A few examples will show that despite their continued presence on the statute book, and despite popular antipathy in general to Papism, their implementation was not robust.

In 1767 Father John Baptiste Malony (or Maloney) was tried at Croydon. He was found guilty of being a priest and condemned to perpetual imprisonment. This was commuted to banishment after a couple of years *by the mercy of the Government.* In 1768 the Reverend James Webb was tried in the Court of the King's Bench for saying Mass, but was acquitted. The Chief Justice, Lord Mansfield, ruled that there was *no evidence sufficient to convict.* In 1769 Dr. James Talbot, coadjutor to Bishop Challoner, was tried for his life at the Old Bailey, on the charge of his Priesthood and of saying Mass. He too was acquitted for lack of evidence. Charles Butler, one of the leading Catholic lawyers of the day, and very much involved in the movement for the repeal of the Penal laws, recounts that around this time one firm of lawyers defended more than twenty priests under prosecutions of this nature.

The International and National Situation

Legislation

The first significant reversal of the trend in anti-Catholic legislation was a direct consequence of England's global territorial expansionist policies. Although in 1771 a Relief Act was passed which allowed Catholics to hold land under lease, with restrictions, the first real acceptance of Catholics as valued and trusted subjects of the realm came in 1774 and was the consequence of war.

The Seven Years War between France and England concluded in 1763 with the Treaty of Paris. France handed over the part of Nouvelle France (New France), called 'Canada' by the French, to the English Crown, who renamed it Quebec after its capital.

Estimates at the time indicated that well over 90% of the 70,000 population were of French origin and mostly Catholic. The wording of the 1774 Act referred *to above sixty-five thousand Persons professing the Religion of the Church of Rome.* Many of these people had roots in Quebec going back for several generations and unsurprisingly they were unwilling to leave. The alternative, of staying as subjects of the British Crown and having to take the Oath of Allegiance, with its explicit affirmation of support for the Protestant Faith, presented an insurmountable impasse. And yet the English Crown needed the loyalty of these new Catholic subjects. They needed it even more as the unrest in the American colonies developed into outright revolution.

Nouvelle-France at its greatest extent, 1712.

The English Province of Quebec, 1774.

The Quebec Act of 1774 gave official recognition to the rights of the Catholic Church in what was termed Lower Canada. The English Government also made territorial claims to Illinois, Indiana, Michigan, Ohio, Wisconsin and parts of Minnesota. Many American Colonists, led by George Washington, had viewed the defeat of the French as a means of expanding further westwards by seizing more lands from the indigenous 'Indian' population.

By declaring the new province of Quebec to be directly under the British Crown, Parliament effectively cut off the territorial expansionist claims of the emerging colonies. Moreover, by replacing an oath of allegiance which made reference to the Protestant Faith, with one that deliberately omitted it, and by guaranteeing free practice of the Catholic Faith, the British government hoped to maintain the loyalty of its new French Catholic subjects. Furthermore French Civil Law was retained in the private arena, though English Common Law was used for public affairs and criminal prosecution. It is worth reproducing and contrasting the wording of the Oath as determined by the 1774 Act to see just how far from the 1559 Elizabethan *Oath of Supremacy* the Crown and British Government were prepared to move in order to maintain the loyalty of the Catholic population.

The 1559 Elizabethan Oath:

I, A. B., do utterly testify and declare in my conscience that the Queen's Highness is the only supreme governor of this realm, and of all other her Highness's dominions and countries, as well in all spiritual or ecclesiastical things or causes, as temporal,

11

and that no foreign prince, person, prelate, state or potentate hath or ought to have any jurisdiction, power, superiority, pre-eminence or authority ecclesiastical or spiritual within this realm; and therefore I do utterly renounce and forsake all foreign jurisdictions, powers, superiorities and authorities, and do promise that from henceforth I shall bear faith and true allegiance to the Queen's Highness, her heirs and lawful successors, and to my power shall assist and defend all jurisdictions, pre-eminences, privileges and authorities granted or belonging to the Queen's Highness, her heirs or successors, or united or annexed to the imperial crown of this realm. So help me God, and by the contents of this Book.

The 1774 Oath:

I A.B. do sincerely promise and swear, That I will be faithful, and bear true Allegiance to his Majesty King George, and him will defend to the utmost of my Power, against all traitorous Conspiracies, and Attempts whatsoever, which shall be made against his Person, Crown. and Dignity; and I will do my utmost Endeavor to disclose and make known to his Majesty, his Heirs and Successors, all Treasons, and traitorous Conspiracies, and Attempts, which I shall know to be against him, or any of them; and all this I do swear without any Equivocation, mental Evasion, or secret Reservation, and renouncing all Pardons and Dispensations from any Power or Person whomsoever to the contrary. So help me GOD.

There are several more paragraphs and statements which emphasise the guaranteed freedom to practise the Catholic religion and which seek to reassure the clergy. One such reads: *... the Clergy of the said Church may hold, receive, and enjoy, their accustomed Dues and Rights, with respect to such Persons only as shall profess the said Religion.*

Here we encounter for the first time in nearly 200 years a reversal of anti-Catholic legislation. Here was *de jure* and *de facto* acknowledgment that Catholicism, far from being a threat to the English Crown, was very much part of the established system. Moreover there was full legal recognition that being a practising Catholic and being a loyal subject of the crown were not irreconcilable.

Acceptance of this principle was to be at the heart of all future legislation relating to the Catholic question in England and Wales.

War

Arguably the wars of the 18th century were among the main driving forces behind the changes in legislation. If the Seven Years War resulted in the first legal recognition that Catholics could be loyal subjects of the Crown abroad, then the American War of Independence, 1775-1782, brought about a revolution in attitudes at home.

Significant numbers of those fighting for King George III were Catholics. Again ten years later, during the wars from 1793 to 1802 against the First French Republic, the British army included Catholics, many from Ireland but also from Scotland and from the New World.

Research has shown the importance at this time of the role of Catholic Irish regiments when Britain was at war with France. These regiments were based at the strategically important locations of Portsmouth and Plymouth, demonstrating acceptance and recognition that Catholic soldiers could be entrusted to be loyal defenders of the realm. In this we encounter a military, as well as a legal, admission that one could be both a loyal subject to the British crown and a practising Catholic. Furthermore, Catholic priests were entitled, legally and openly, to carry out a Catholic ministry in these regiments.

But before similar liberalisation could be extended to the whole country and the civilian population in general, the Law had to be amended, and, as we shall see, this was not always a straightforward process.

First Catholic Relief Act, 1778

As indicated above, anti-Papist legislation in England and Wales, if not ignored, was no longer being rigorously enforced. Consequently a large number of the Catholic gentry, fearful of drawing attention to themselves, opposed reform or repeal of the anti-Catholic Acts of 1689 and 1700. They suspected that any such move would arouse anti-Catholic feelings and regenerate old suspicions as to their political intentions.

We have, however, seen that 'home' legislation was out of step with that which governed Catholics in some Crown territories abroad and that large numbers of Catholics comprised an integral part of the military within the British Isles. The question arose as to whether these recruits should take the Elizabethan Oath of Allegiance. There were undoubtedly several paradoxes in the existing situation.

The Jacobite Risings between 1688 and 1745 aimed at returning the deposed House of Stuart to the English throne. Following the Glorious Revolution of 1688, the Protestant, William of Orange was declared monarch. However James II, and, after his death in 1701, his son, James Charles Edward, continued to lay claim to the thrones of England and Scotland. With the death of Queen Anne in in 1714, George, Prince Elector of Hanover, was declared King George I of Great Britain and Ireland. There were several other claimants to the throne, the strongest claim being that of James Stuart.

However the 1701 Act of Settlement prohibited Catholics from ascending to the throne. This led directly to the so called 1715 Jacobite Rising and its subsequent defeat. The Stuarts, and with them many Catholics, did not abandon their claim. They saw another opportunity to rebel in 1744. The English army was depleted as many troops were engaged in hostilities in Europe, on account of the War of the Austrian Succession. However the 1745 Rising ended in the overwhelming defeat of the Jacobite forces at Culloden in April 1746.

Following the failure of the '45 Rebellion, Charles Stuart, the Young Pretender, son of James, allied himself with the French during the Seven Years' War of 1756-1763. Although this came to nothing, owing, as reported at the time, to Charles' *unruly stubborn behaviour and reported drunkenness* at the French Court, the Stuarts, and their supporters in the British Isles, retained their claim to the throne. This was an embarrassment to many Englishmen, both Catholic and Protestant, and a stumbling block to forming a working relationship between English Catholics and the Crown.

On the death of James Stuart, the Old Pretender, in 1766, the Pope refused to recognise his son Charles as the heir to the English throne, accepting the Hanoverians and their descendants as legitimate rulers of Britain and Ireland. This in effect overturned the Bull, *Regnans in Excelsis*, issued, as we saw, during the reign of Elizabeth. For the first time in about 200 years Catholics in Britain were no longer being required by their spiritual leader to be enemies of the state. Negotiations could be opened for the repeal of the penal laws.

Supported by the Government and several leading parliamentarians, Sir George Savile introduced the Bill which became the 1778 Act for Catholic Relief. This sought to address some of the existing legal contradictions.

The new Act imposed an Oath which declared loyalty to the reigning sovereign and rejected the claims of the Pretender. The Act required Catholics to repudiate certain doctrines regarding Papal temporal rights attributed to them dating from the Papal Bull of 1570. We saw how Pope Pius V had issued this edict in the wake of the rebellion of the Northern Earls against Elizabeth of 1567-8, declaring Elizabeth a heretic, and therefore excommunicate. In medieval theory, an excommunicated monarch could not lawfully reign, and his subjects were entitled to withdraw their allegiance. It was even argued that an excommunicated prince could be lawfully murdered. Linked with this was the claim that the Pope had temporal as well as spiritual jurisdiction in England. The 1778 Act repeatedly required Catholics to reject any such claims. In the process of amending the Penal Laws, most important was the repeal of those sections of the 1698 and 1700 Acts referring to the *taking and prosecuting of priests*.

The penalty of perpetual imprisonment for keeping a Catholic school was likewise abolished. Catholics were allowed to inherit and purchase land. The Act also boosted the recruitment of Catholic soldiers and sailors. This was not only a significant factor in easing the shortfall of manpower in the military but, as we shall see, became pivotal in the reasoning for total Catholic Emancipation over the next half century.

The Gordon Riots, 1780

However, as feared by many of the English Catholic gentry, there was a backlash and it came in the shape of the Protestant Association. This had been created in 1780, with Lord George Gordon as its President, to force the repeal of the 1778 Act.

The American War of Independence was at its height and Gordon feared that large numbers of Catholics in the British military would be a danger to the Crown. He argued that they would join forces with their co-religionists on the Continent and attack Britain. Having succeeded in preventing the 1778 Act becoming law in Scotland, he believed he could achieve the same success in England. During 1780 he had several audiences with George III, but Gordon's eccentricities and increasingly erratic behaviour compelled the King to deny him any further audiences. Apart from his anti-Papist stance Gordon also advocated the return of absolute monarchical rule. George III saw this as tantamount to a reversal of the constitutional settlement of 1688. He feared that any such move might even jeopardise his position as monarch.

Among the masses, however, Gordon certainly received a great deal of support. On the 29th of May 1780 he called a meeting of the Protestant Association. Four days later, on the 2nd of June, he led a crowd of around 50,000 people who marched in procession from St George's Fields to the Houses of Parliament. Their aim was to present a petition demanding the repeal of the 1787 Relief Act. The House of Commons rejected the petition by 192 votes to 6.

The 'Gordon Riots' continued for several days. The mob destroyed some Catholic chapels attached to embassies, ransacked the homes of known Catholics, set fire to Newgate prison and attacked the Bank of England and other public buildings. Finally the riot was suppressed by the army. Some reports say that as many as 285 people were shot dead and another 200 wounded. The consequences of these riots were far reaching both at home and abroad. They destabilised relations with several foreign powers such as Spain and Austria. These were Catholic countries which viewed the upsurge of anti-Catholicism with alarm.

At home the riots caused dissention between those who favoured Catholic Relief, such as the followers of John Wilkes, who had led troops in the suppression of the riot, and those who opposed reform of the methods of policing. Suggestions were made that a national police force should be created. Many argued that this was anti-liberal and authoritarian. The debate split the reforming wing of English politics. The reaction among Catholics was one of alarm. The worst fears of those gentry who had argued against 'Relief' appeared to have been vindicated. Even if the Law sought to accept that Catholics could be loyal subjects, the riots showed that a large section of the public distrusted Catholicism.

As for Gordon, his relationship with the establishment became increasingly strained. He was accused of high treason, imprisoned, in some comfort, in the Tower and subsequently released. In 1786 he was excommunicated by the Archbishop of Canterbury. In 1787 he was accused of defaming Marie Antoinette, the French Ambassador and the administration of Justice in England. He fled to the Netherlands but was returned to England where he was found guilty and given a five year prison sentence. Whilst in Newgate Prison he converted to Judaism and insisted on living as a strict Orthodox Jew. He died in prison of typhoid fever in 1792 at 42 years of age.

The Debate within Catholicism in England

In 1782 the *Catholic Committee* was re-instituted. This organisation had its origins in the *Catholic Association*, founded in July 1756 by Charles O'Conor of Belanagare, John Curry, and Thomas Wyse: Catholics whose family fortunes had suffered greatly under the penal laws. Whereas its predecessor had a specifically Irish focus, the new Committee was formed by English landed gentry. It was an attempt to mitigate the effects of the Gordon Riots and the feelings that lay behind them. Its leading members were Lord Petre and Sir John Throckmorton. Members of Lord Petre's family had supported the Jacobite cause and some had been executed for their part in the two uprisings of 1715 and 1745.

In 1782 Charles Butler became Secretary of the Catholic Committee. He was a practising lawyer, with chambers in Lincoln's Inn. In 1788 he was asked by the Committee to draft a new Relief Bill. Butler had been educated at the English College in Douai and on his return to England studied law. He married Mary Eyston a member of the East Hendred recusant family and granddaughter of Charles Eyston the Antiquary. As a Catholic, Butler could not be called to the bar but was able to practise as a conveyancer. Keen to have the Penal Laws removed, he worked in the Committee for this end.

The debate within Catholic ranks focused on the power of the bishops, their temporal authority and the role of the Papacy in their appointment. Butler sided with those who maintained it was in order for Catholics to deny that the Pope could exercise temporal power, and produced, in 1788, a 'declaration' to this effect. The intention of the 'declaration' was to reassure Protestants fearful of a resurgence of Catholic aspirations regarding Papal authority in England. Lord Stanhope, an Anglican, worked with Butler on a 'Protestation' disclaiming any intention by Catholics of supporting the authority of the Papacy in England.

This was in direct contrast to the Ultramontanists, who supported the superiority of the Papacy over the authority of local temporal or spiritual hierarchies. At first three of the Vicars Apostolic and 240 priests signed the declaration. However, the following year, fearing unacceptable compromise, the Vicars Apostolic condemned an oath proposed by the Catholic Committee. This latter aspect of the Act was seen by the Vicars Apostolic, who at this time administered the Catholic Church in England, as tampering with matters of ecclesiastical discipline. This stance brought Butler into conflict with John Milner, later Bishop Milner.

The 1791 Catholic Relief Act

This is such a significant Act that it is worth reproducing its main terms.

1.   No Catholic taking the Oath was henceforward to be prosecuted for being a Papist or for being educated in Catholicism, or for hearing Catholic Mass or saying it, or for being a priest or deacon or for entering into, or belonging to, any ecclesiastical order or community in the Church of Rome, or for assisting at, or performing, any Catholic rites or ceremonies.
2.   Catholics were no longer to be summoned to take the Oath of Supremacy, or to be removed from London; the legislation of King George I, requiring them to register their estates and wills, was absolutely repealed; while the professions of counsellor and barrister at law, attorney, solicitor, and notary were opened to them.
3.   It was, however, provided that all their assemblies for religious worship should be certified at Quarter Sessions; that no person should officiate at such assembly until his name had been recorded by the Clerk of the Peace: that no such place of assembly should be locked or barred during the meeting; and that the building in which it was held, should not have a steeple or bell.

English Catholics were still divided over the issue of 'ecclesiastical interference' in matters which many considered beyond the jurisdiction of their Church leaders. The feud survived and was proclaimed to the world by the formation in 1792 of the Cisalpine Club, whose members were pledged *to resist any ecclesiastical interference which may militate against the freedom of English Catholics.* This consisted mainly of the members of the Catholic Committee but was extended to about fifty more like-minded Catholics.

It may be useful at this point to explain the two terms, *Cisalpine* and *Ultramontane*, which were frequently used in the debate concerning the role of the Papacy in England. 'Cisalpine' literally means *this side of the Alps*. It refers to those who believed that control of the Catholic Church in England should be retained within the national borders of England, acknowledging the need for a working inter-relationship between Crown and Parliament. A practical example concerned the question of the right of the British government to veto nominations by Rome to the position of bishop. The 'Ultramontane' view, *beyond the mountains*, claimed that the Papacy possessed certain inalienable rights in the governance of the Catholic Church and Catholics. There were therefore areas, it was claimed, where the national government had no powers. Among these were the rights of the Papacy to nominate and appoint Bishops without state interference. This was a cause of major dissension within the Catholic ranks. There was also the related question of the Royal Veto on the appointment of Bishops in Ireland, which it was proposed to confer on the English Government. This aspect of the narrative belongs chiefly to the history of Emancipation in Ireland, but the issue underlines the fundamental problems faced by pro-reforming parties at the time.

The main tenet of the Cisalpine Club was that, although in union with Rome, English Catholics should retain a certain independence. To a large extent this was the consequence of nearly 200 years of isolation. During this time the Church had been supported and managed by a small but powerful group of lay Catholics, who had become accustomed to finding an accommodation with the State in a hostile legal environment. The Club met about five times a year to dine and discuss further Catholic relief.

In time the 'Cisalpine' aspect receded and it became simply a dining club. The involvement of Catholic laity was viewed with alarm by some of the Catholic hierarchy. It was a division that resurfaced in the negotiations for Catholic relief in the early 1800s. It came to the fore again when the members of the Oxford Movement, during the 1830s and '40s, wished to accentuate the role of the Anglo-Catholic tradition.

Despite these problems, both from within Catholic ranks and from the suspicions and fears of the Protestant establishment, there is no doubt that the 1791 Act effectively removed anti-Catholic legislation from the law of the land. There were still many areas of civil rights that required addressing, such as the right to hold certain high public offices. However, in practice, Catholics could now gather and worship openly and legally, they could educate their youth, they could train their clergy, they could own property and pass this on to their heirs.

In the next chapter we shall now see how the Catholics of Reading and the surrounding area took full and immediate advantage of these reforms, but we shall also see that the tensions and differences within the Catholic community played a role in shaping the Church we know today.

PART 2

The Return of Catholicism to Reading,

1790 – 1817.

CHAPTER 1

Catholicism in Reading and the Surrounding Area in the Late 18th Century

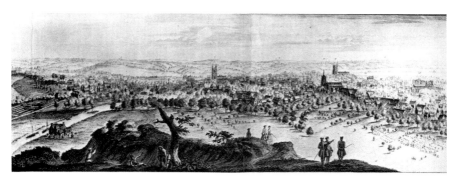

1734 print of Reading from the South by Samuel and Nathaniel Buck. Courtesy of Reading Library

Towards the end of the 18th Century virtually all the landed gentry in the area around Reading were Catholics. There were Catholic families at Whiteknights to the South, Englefield and Ufton Court to the West, Mapledurham, Stonor and Britwell to the North, and, with the arrival of the Whebles at Woodley Lodge, also to the East. Despite this, recusancy records indicate that the Catholic population was very small indeed. We know, for instance, that Franciscan priests served as chaplains at Whiteknights but that their congregations were often in single figures.

These Franciscan friars included Philip Lorraine, around 1765, Richard Bonaventure Healy from 1773 to 1775, Edward Madew in1782 and George Athanasius Baynham between 1783 and 1794. Fr. Baynham also served at Ufton Court.

We saw above how the Catholic Committee, formed by Catholic gentry in 1787, became highly influential in the reform movement. The leaders of this group included members of families well known in the Reading area. They included Charles Butler, whose wife was Mary Eyston, Sir Henry Charles Englefield and Sir John Throckmorton.

Reading and the 1791 Relief Act

The passing of the 1791 Relief Act had immediate consequences in Reading and the surrounding area, as well as for the rest of the country. In the previous chapter we saw that the Act allowed assemblies for Catholic worship provided that they had been certified at Quarter Sessions. In other words Catholics could legally have places of worship where Mass could be said. Contrast this with the prosecution for the capital offence of saying Mass that Dr James Talbot had faced only 22 years earlier. It is interesting that the Act stated that these places of worship could not have spires, towers or bells, they were not registered for marriages, and burials were not permitted within their grounds. Doors could not be barred or locked during services.

As an immediate consequence of the Act, Father Ballass of Woolhampton and Father Baynam of Ufton Court applied for, and were granted, licenses for a *chapel or place of religious worship for persons professing the Roman catholic religion.* This was on the 10th of January 1792. There is some evidence that Michael Blount of Mapledurham, in 1791, built one of the first 'legal chapels' in England since the Reformation.

Records show that small numbers of Catholics living on the various estates mentioned above attended Mass. The Relief Acts of 1778 and 1791 brought about a new openness and a consequent gradual increase in numbers.

Reading Town and Anna Maria Smart

We have seen that Mass was being said around Reading. What about within Reading town itself?

When looking at the history of Catholicism in Reading at this time, one name, that of Smart, Mrs. Anna Maria Smart in particular, stands out. Born Anna Maria Carnan, she was the daughter of Mary Carnan (née Hounshill) whose husband, William, had been the proprietor of the *Oxford Gazette and Reading Mercury.* They had two other children, Thomas and John. William Carnan died in 1737, leaving his business to his colleague John Newbery. John married Mary, so becoming Anna Maria's stepfather. He died in 1767 leaving the business, in part, to Anna Maria.

Before proceeding to examine the role Anna Maria played in the resurgence of Catholicism in Reading, it would be useful to look more closely at her life and at her relationships with her stepfather John Newbery and her husband Christopher Smart.

John Newbery was born in 1716 at Waltham St. Lawrence. He is known as a publisher, author and bookseller. He worked for William Carnan and, as mentioned, inherited his business in 1737. In 1744 he set up a bookshop and publishing house in London. In 1765 it became one of the first, if not the first, to publish specifically children's books, including *A Little Pretty Pocket-Book* and *Little Goody Two-Shoes.* The Newberys' home was at Canonbury House, Islington. Newbery himself was a literary man but above all an entrepreneur. It is not clear whether he wrote, or merely published, the works of children's literature for which he is remembered, not least by the children's literary medal named after him. He published a miscellany of works and also set up and ran several reviews and periodicals such as *The Student* and *TheMidwife*. He not only came into contact with, but was also respected by, the leading literary and cultural figures of the day. Among his friends he could count Dr. Johnson, Thomas Arne, Oliver Goldsmith and Charles Burney. His business was based at *The Bible and Sun* in St Paul's Churchyard: the centre of publishing in the London of the 17th and 18th centuries

In addition to the three children by her first marriage, Mary had two more children with John. The first was a daughter, Mary, born in 1742, who later married a Catholic wine merchant, Michael Power. Their second child was a boy, but tragedy was to strike the young family when he died in 1751 after a long illness.

It is worth noting the harmony in which this couple lived. One was a staunch Catholic, the other a committed Protestant. That such relationships, though not common, were not unusual, is demonstrated by the fact that they agreed to follow the accepted convention of the day, namely that boys were to be brought up in the father's religion and girls in the mother's. So Anna Maria was a Catholic whilst her brothers, Thomas and John, were Protestants. When Mary and John had their own children this same pattern was adhered to.

It was into this bustling, literary world that Christopher Smart entered, and sought to make his name and fortune.

Christopher Smart holding a copy of one of Pope's poems that he translated.

Anna Maria, a Catholic, married Christopher Smart in 1752 or possibly 1753. She herself claimed the earlier date. Partly because of Smart's position at Cambridge, so that he could continue to receive the money from his Fellowship, the marriage was kept secret. The added complication was Anna Maria's Catholicism. It is likely that the *clandestine marriage,* as their daughter Elizabeth later called it, was a Catholic one and that it took place at St Mary's, Moorfields, the centre for Catholics living around Islington. Unfortunately the records held in St Mary's were destroyed a few years later in the Gordon Riots. The wedding probably took place before the Hardwicke Act of 1753 which required all marriages to be registered by an Anglican clergyman.

Christopher was a Fellow of Pembroke Hall, Cambridge, and so, some have argued, possibly in Anglican orders. As early as 1749 Smart had left Cambridge to earn his living as a writer in London. Even so Cambridge continued to value him and send him money. The College did not deprive him of his Fellowship until constrained to do so when the marriage became public. College members were not allowed to be married. Note that he had left Cambridge to live in London before he met Anna Maria. Some commentators have claimed that Smart only moved from Cambridge after, and because of, his marriage to Anna Maria. This is clearly not the case.

In London Smart met with John Newbery who began by publishing some of his works, the first being *Horatian Canons of Friendship*. Smart and Newbery evidently became close friends as well as business associates. Newbery made Smart a partner in his magazine, *The Student*. Soon they began producing a monthly magazine, *The Midwife,* which featured a witch and midwife called Mary Midnight. This dreadful old lady passed satirical comment on the political and social issues of the day. She was especially concerned with the state of marriage and even became a soothsayer, describing the England of future years such as 1931. At the same time Smart was writing serious poetry and won the Seaton Prize at Cambridge in three consecutive years.

Christopher suffered from bouts of insanity and was possibly an alcoholic. He was unsuccessful in earning a living from his writings, although he was well respected as a writer at the time and some of his books are still in print. He was admired by Goldsmith and Pope, whose works he translated into Latin.

There has been much discussion about Smart's insanity, about the form it took and its extent. Christopher Devlin's book, *Poor Kit Smart,* traces this aspect of Smart's life. One thing is clear: Smart's confinements were not of the dreadful Bedlam variety. He was treated by Dr Battie, who was a pioneer in the treatment of mental illness. Physical restraint was kept to the absolute minimum and the repulsive spectacle of 'visitors' who abused the inmates physically, as well as verbally, was totally forbidden. Smart lived in comfortable surroundings whilst under Dr Battie's care. His possible second place of confinement, in Chelsea, is not so well documented but again it was in a private establishment. Smart himself considered it a prison and praised *** (sic) *who was influential* in his release. There can be little doubt that Smart suffered some form of mental illness. It was centred on his religious belief that he had a mission to reform the Church of England. His poetry became increasingly focused on this issue. He also became estranged from his wife, Anna Maria, whom he could no longer support financially.

Consequently in 1759 or 1760 Anna Maria took her two daughters to stay with relatives in Ireland. Smart found himself in the debtors' prison at least twice, though thanks to his brother-in-law, Thomas Carnan, he lived after 1768 under 'Rules of the King's Bench', i.e. not under strict confinement. Several friends helped pay his expenses. Among those we know of is Charles Burney. Other notable literary figures who admired him and supported him financially were Dr Johnson and David Garrick. Smart died impoverished and probably insane in 1771. Arguably his main fame today lies in the poem, still in print, about his cat Jeoffrey.

CHAPTER 2

The Reading Mercury

Smart and Cowslade: Publishers and Printers

We have seen that Anna Maria and Christopher had two children, Mary Anne, or Marianne as she is often called, and Elizabeth Anne. By 1760 Anna Maria and her two daughters were to be found in Dublin. It would appear that she stayed with Kit Smart's sister, also called Marianne, and her husband Richard Falkiner, a Dublin barrister. She returned to England and settled in Reading in 1762. This is a significant date in the history of Catholicism in Reading as it marks the beginning of a period of nearly 80 years where the main presses of the town were owned by Catholics.

John Newbery had in all likelihood already given Anna Maria some financial support. In 1762 it appears that the ownership of the *Reading Mercury* (which I shall refer to as the *Mercury*), changed hands. On the 25th of January 1762 the first issue of the new series of the paper was published and it stated; *the property of this paper is somewhat changed and the conduct of it conveyed to another hand (i.e. A M Smart) who is to be considered its Author.*

The publishers are listed as Anna Maria Smart and Company at the Bible and Crown, Market Place, Reading. The printers are given as John Carnan and Company, also in Market Place. The name *Bible and Crown* was that given to the premises of the *Mercury* and was situated on the southerly wing of Sutton's Seeds' offices in Market Place. The premises not only housed the *Mercury*, but functioned as general store selling wallpaper, tobacco, snuff, herbs and a host of 'quack medicines'.

From 1762, under Mrs Smart's and her brother John's management, the paper increased in size and circulation, becoming a respected and influential journal. However these were not easy times for the press. The price of producing newspapers was steadily increasing as the Tory administration of Lord North imposed various taxes and duties. For instance in 1776 an additional half-penny in the Stamp Duty was imposed. Four years later, in May 1780, an additional six pence was added to the Advertising Duty. This brought the basic charge for advertisements to four shillings and sixpence. In 1792 the paper's size was increased to five columns. As the price of paper came under pressure, following increased excise duty, so too the cost of each copy increased, first to threepence-halfpenny and, in 1794, to fourpence. In 1797 the price again increased to sixpence following yet another increase in Excise Duty.

Other minor administrative changes occurred when Newbery's colourful name for the shop in Market Place, *The Bible and Crown,* was no longer used. Finding compositors and printers also appeared to be a problem. In 1776, John Carnan placed an advertisement for an apprentice: *A sober youth of docile disposition, who has had a grammatical education, is wanted as an apprentice at the Printing Office in Reading. He will have the advantage of being entitled to the Freedom of the City of London. A Handsome premium will be expected.*

We don't know whether this post was filled or, if so, by whom. We do have records of at least two other printers working in the *Mercury* offices. One was 'Honest' John Copeland, who died in 1801, aged eighty-two, after about 60 years of service. He worked at the onerous task of 'pressman' until shortly before his death. Another long-term employee was Benjamin Candles who, after serving as compositor for fifty years, died in 1810.

Reading Mercury Offices in Market Place. Courtesy of Reading Library

The Mercury offices are the nearest of the frontages of the third building on the right.

These details give us a little insight into what must have been the nature of the paper and its staff. At this distance in time, and without written records or diaries, we can only make speculative assumptions about relationships within the firm. It is reasonable, however, to assume good management and a degree of contentment when employees stayed this long in a business requiring a great deal of skill. The consequent prestige enjoyed by such workers meant that they would have been in considerable demand elsewhere. It is also likely that close friendships and camaraderie must have developed between proprietors and workers.

The Cowslade Family 1783 - 1811

In 1785 with the unexpected death of Anna Maria's brother John, after a paralytic stroke, his share of the paper was divided between his two nieces: Anna Maria's daughters, Marianne and Elizabeth Anne. In 1783 or 1784 Marianne married Thomas Cowslade, who had been assisting Anna Maria in the running of the business. As a result of the marriage Thomas took over the management of her side of the business, which he shared with his mother-in-law, Anna Maria.

Marianne Cowslade   Thomas Cowslade

The name Cowslade is pivotal to the subsequent history of the return of Catholicism in Reading. The *Mercury* is also one the most reliable primary sources for any history of Reading at this time and for the next hundred years. The paper stayed in the Cowslade family until the death of Thomas' grandson, William Wallace Cowslade, in 1915, at the age of eighty, as a result of a riding accident. So it is fitting to examine the origins of the Cowslades.

The family came from near Newbury. Another Thomas, a cousin of Marianne's husband, invented a method of turning bindweed stalks into corduroy. Yet another cousin was a Gentleman Usher at Court. Thomas himself was Quartermaster of the Reading Corps of Volunteers and in 1805 was promoted to the rank of Captain.

Although the ownership of the paper remained in the joint partnership of Anna Maria and Thomas, the Cowslade name is omitted after 1798. This would appear not so much due to a change in the legal ownership of the paper but rather because Thomas took to running the shop, whilst Anna Maria managed the newspaper. The shop was primarily a bookshop and stationers, but it continued to stock quack medicines as well as offering bookbinding and bespoke small-scale printing. Towards the end of the 1800s Thomas took on the agency for several insurance companies including the *Phoenix*. The shop also became a central collecting point for various charities. These included aid for imprisoned debtors, the Danish prisoners of war and the Reading Soup and Coal Charities. In 1801 Thomas was appointed Postmaster for Reading and the Mercury Office became the Reading Post Office.

Quite unexpectedly, according to all reports, Thomas committed suicide in December 1806, leaving Marianne with nine, or possibly ten, young children. The exact sequence of events and the reasons why Thomas took his own life are a mystery. *The Gentleman's Magazine*, Vol. 76, reported that he died: *By shooting himself with a pistol, in Andover market-place (on 30th December 1806) ...He was a man universally respected and no cause can be assigned for his committing suicide. Verdict Insanity*

The *Mercury* does not make any direct reference to the incident. Anna Maria now carried on as sole proprietor of the newspaper until her own death in 1809, aged seventy-seven. The *Mercury* printed her obituary, reproduced below, on 22 May 1809. Her influence in restoring Catholic worship to Reading was greater than that of any other individual.

In her own right, as a business partner with her son-in-law and most of all as mother to both her daughters, who themselves were to such a great extent instrumental in the establishment of the Catholic community, she is a person who should be remembered and honoured. In many ways she was a remarkably modern woman. She was a single parent who had to raise her children without their father, Christopher Smart. She had been forced to seek refuge abroad, in Ireland, with her in-laws. She retuned to England and had to learn to run a business. As we shall see she established the first Catholic Mass centre in Reading since the Reformation. With her daughters she arranged accommodation for the French refugee priests. She suffered the agony, whatever the reason, of her son-in-law's suicide. Most significantly she laid a solid foundation for an informative press for the townspeople of Reading. This last achievement, in the face of rising costs, mainly through taxation and the fear of revolution, is one that in itself merits admiration.

Through all these hardships she maintained her Catholic faith and, no doubt, enhanced the prestige of Catholics, helping to overcome deep-rooted prejudices in an otherwise hostile environment. Anna Maria likewise deserves due recognition as one of the country's first businesswomen.

The *Mercury* reported her death in these words: *Mrs Smart enjoyed many years a fine state of health ... She settled her accounts on the eve of her decease, and was attempting to rise when she expired ... A Catholic in religion, a Christian in true spirit of the Character, she never enquired the principles of anyone who solicited her help ... The great service she rendered the French Emigrants being so well known ... to assist Foreigners conspicuously requires fortitude no less than Benevolence.* (See Appendix B for a full transcript of Mrs Smart's obituary)

With the death of Anna Maria in 1809, the ownership of the paper passed in its entirety to Marianne and Elizabeth.

Marianne Smart and Elizabeth Lenoir

In 1795 Elizabeth had married a French émigré nobleman, Jean Baptiste Le Noir (sometimes spelt Lenoir) de la Brosse, Chevalier of the Royal and Military Order of St. Louis. He had lost most of his property as a result of the French Revolution. On coming to England he settled in Reading where he earned a meagre living teaching French. Elizabeth and Jean Baptiste had no children. There are some hints that Le Noir had in fact been married in France, bringing his two daughters with him to England. To date it has not been possible to verify this nor discover what happened to his first wife. Jean Baptiste died in 1833, aged 80.

Elizabeth became known as a writer of some renown. Her works as a novelist and poet were admired by Dr. Burney and Mary Russell Mitford. Elizabeth died on the 6th of May 1841, aged 86, at the Priory, Caversham where, with one her nieces, she ran a school for young ladies.

The Priory, Caversham. Courtesy of Reading Library

Anna Maria Smart had set a precedent in the town. It was unusual for a woman at this time not only to be a proprietor of a major business but in addition to undertake its administration. Now the people of Reading found themselves with two ladies in charge of their local newspaper. In 1811 Francis, Marianne's son, joined them as co-proprietor. Nevertheless the paper's editor remained one of the two sisters. As both could claim literary prowess we are not sure which. One could surmise that it was probably Marianne, as Elizabeth, we know, ran her school in Caversham.

29

Francis Cowslade: Joint Proprietor 1811 - 1830, Editor 1830 – 1834

We have just seen that Francis Cowslade became joint proprietor of the *Mercury* in 1811. Under his influence the paper's anti-Tory attitude gradually became more explicit, so much so that it became known as an overtly Whig journal. In 1818 the *Mercury* supported proposals for the formation of a *Reading Purity of Election Society*. In essence this was part of the national campaign for electoral reform and the abolition of rotten boroughs. In the same year the paper backed the Whig candidate, Mr. Palmer.

At the 1826 election the *Mercury* again supported the reforming Whig cause. This time there were two Independent candidates who in fact had reforming Whig tendencies: Mr. Palmer and Mr. Berkeley Monck.

We know that when Marianne died in 1830, full management passed to her son, Francis. He died in 1834, but, despite the brevity of his tenure as sole proprietor and editor, his involvement in the struggle for Parliamentary Reform meant he played a significant role in Reading in the passing of the Great Reform Act of 1832. He intensified the paper's campaign with frequent editorials supporting Reform. In the same year he linked up with the *London Sun*. Francis used what amounted to syndicated Reform news from this paper, making it immediately available to the people of Reading.

The rejection of the 1830 Reform Bill by the House of Lords was condemned by the *Mercury*, whereas its final acceptance in 1832 elicited a special celebratory supplement, much of whose material came from the *London Sun*. His stance is not surprising. Despite its avowed neutrality the *Mercury* had always been politically on the 'liberal' wing. For instance as far back as 1774 it congratulated the *friends of freedom and independence* who had *nominated and elected Francis Annesley, a gentleman in the strictest sense independent.*

It was most fitting, therefore, that Francis was presented with a large, solid silver, loving cup or bowl in recognition of the *Mercury's* services to the cause of electoral reform. It bore the inscription:

As a token of gratitude for the gratuitous information afforded at all times to the public life, this Piece of Plate is presented by the Mechanics of Reading to Mr Francis Peter Cowslade, Editor of the Reading Mercury. A.D.1832.

Following the death of Francis, ownership passed to his brother Frederic. In 1839 his brother Henry Hartley joined him as co-proprietor. It is not clear what Elizabeth Lenoir's role was. She had become joint proprietor with her sister in 1809 but does not appear to have taken an active role. Her obituary, in May 1841, makes no mention of this aspect of her life.

In 1841 we know, from census records, that Frederic was living at the *Mercury* offices in 6 Market Place. Others mentioned are Anne (née Walpole, his wife), aged 40, Marianah (sic) aged 13 and John aged seven months. The manner in which the *Mercury* brought weekly accounts to the people of Reading regarding political and military developments throughout Europe, is worthy of further comment and this is an aspect of or story that we shall look at in a later chapter.

CHAPTER 3

The First Mass Centres in Reading since the Reformation

Minster Street Mission Chapel , 1789

When Mrs. Smart first came to Reading in 1762, or thereabouts, there were few registered Catholics in the town. However we do have a record in 1767 of 13 'Papists' being resident in the Parish of St Lawrence.

Sex	Age	Occupation
Man	64	Cutler
Man	16	
Woman	40	Bookseller
Man	60	Flax dresser
Woman	50	His wife
Man	75	Gentleman
Woman	42	Wife of an Actor
Woman	20	Her daughter
Woman	33	Wife of a Maltster
Man	38	Printer
Woman	24	Servant
Woman	55	Washerwoman
Man	25	Blacksmiths

Mrs Smart attended Mass at Whiteknights and Mapledurham as there was nowhere in Reading where Mass was said. Doubtlessly as a consequence of this inconvenience, and as a person with great organising skills, she determined to address the situation. It is not surprising therefore to learn that she made arrangements for Mass to be said in Reading town itself.

Consequently by 1789, certainly before the 1791 Act, Mrs Smart rented a room in Minster St. so that Mass could be said. It would appear that this was a regular but infrequent arrangement and that Fr. Baynam, the Franciscan priest, would come occasionally to say Mass there.

However with the outbreak of the French Revolution the landlord of the Minster Street house one day accosted Elizabeth Smart, telling her to stop Mass being said. The story comes from a document known as the *Cowslade Manuscript*. This was written by one of Elizabeth's nieces, probably Eleanor, around 1841. It describes the rebirth of Catholicism in Reading from the 18th century, drawing on family records and memories. .

Minster Street 1828.

Courtesy of Reading Library

Eleanor reports the incident in the following words, (the underlinings are in the original):

She (Elizabeth Smart) *was abruptly stopped by the master of the house saying to her 'You cannot <u>perform</u> here this morning'. Recovering from her surprise she answered 'Why not?' He rejoined: 'Because my wife is in child birth and she cannot be delivered while you are <u>performing.</u>' To this Miss Smart made no other reply than by lifting the latch of the Chapel door, on which the landlord exclaimed in a threatening tone: 'If you attempt to perform, I will disturb you.' Miss Smart, while her heart was dying within her, answered resolutely: 'Do so at your peril'. Renewing his threat, the man retired. The service began and went on without interruption beyond the sound of vessels being emptied with the accompaniment of offensive smells which passed for accidental with all the Congregation but one, who, as soon as the service was over proceeded to carry into effect the plan she had formed in the course of it.*

Mass was never said again at this location as Elizabeth put her plan into action and sought out an alternative, more secure, venue and one that was to prove significant in the history of Catholicism in Reading.

Finch's Buildings: The Mission Chapel, Hosier Lane, 1791 – 1811

In 1791, when she was 36 or 37 years old, Elizabeth Anne acquired the tenement of part of Finch's Buildings on the south side of Hosier Lane, later called Hosier Street. At the time Hosier Lane reached well beyond its current limits, more or less following the line of today's Baker Street. It was cut off by the IDR in the 20th century. The wording concerning the nature of the ownership is ambiguous. It refers to Elizabeth 'acquiring' the property using money from a recent legacy. It is not clear whether she bought the freehold, the leasehold or even just rented it.

Finch's Buildings showing individual plots as referred to in the Cowslade Manuscript.

Courtesy of Reading Library

Finch's Buildings had belonged to Lady Vachel (or Vatchel) whose family, according to the *Catholic Registers of Reading* compiled by Scantlebury, had been known recusants from Elizabethan times. Elizabeth Smart converted an upper room into a chapel which was capable of holding about 170 people. This in itself gives us an indication regarding the number of Catholics in the town at the time. However international events, the French Revolution and the ensuing war between France and Britain soon boosted the town's population and many of these incomers were Catholics. Some were foreigners fleeing Revolutionary France. The influx of troops, including regiments containing a strong Irish element, likewise added to the number. We have seen, however, that these now had their own chaplains.

The room at Finch's Buildings was to serve the Catholics of Reading from 1791 to 1811. The number of Catholics in the town increased significantly over this same period. It was the first legal Catholic Mass centre and Mission in Reading since the Reformation, and was the forerunner of the current Catholic Parish in the centre of Reading. Finch's Buildings not only provided a secure base for weekly Mass but also offered a house for the priests serving the community, as well as a place where visitors and guests could be offered a welcome and refuge.

In the midst of this turmoil Elizabeth had heard from friends in France that four French priests from the Rouen diocese were in Dover waiting to be offered refuge. According to the *Cowslade Manuscript,* both of Anna Maria's daughters, Marianne and Elizabeth Anne, had spent three years of their early life at the Ursuline Convent in Boulogne for their education. There are different accounts of how the priests arrived. The more dramatic of these is that they appeared one dark and stormy evening at the *Mercury's* offices in Market Place and Elizabeth escorted them, under the cover of darkness, to Finch's Buildings.

Finch's Buildings, previously Lady Vatchel's Dower house.
Courtesy of Reading Library

Thanks to the *Cowslade Manuscript* we know the names of these priests. They were the Abbés Loriot, Miard de la Blardière, Godquin and Gondré. One report says that another fifth priest, Monsieur le Doyen, joined this community shortly afterwards. This interpretation is probably incorrect. The *Doyen* or *Dean* is a title of a superior in a community and it is more likely that the Dean of Rouen was making a tour of England to see how his priests were faring around the country. *Cowslade* reports that: *The Dean and the priests who had followed him to Reading were sent to their destinations and of the occupants of Finch's buildings, five only remained.*

There is obviously a query as to how many priests actually did remain in Reading. We only have the names of four until the arrival of François Longuet in 1802.

We do have a report that vestments and furnishings were obtained from the vacated Englefield chapel. In 1794 Father Baynam had moved to Ufton Court following the sale of the Whiteknight's Estate to Henry Addington, later Viscount Sidmouth, who became Prime Minister. But far more wide reaching developments were to impact on the development of the emerging Catholic community in Reading following revolution, war and persecution in what must have seemed a 'far away country'.

In the next section of this work we shall look in more detail at how the French Revolution unfolded, how this impacted upon the town of Reading, how it was reported in the *Mercury* and how it led directly to the creation of a congregation which was to become the modern Parish of St. James and St William of York.

PART 3

THE FRENCH REVOLUTION

AND

READING

CHAPTER 1

Revolution in France 1789 -1793

The Revolution as Reported by the Reading Mercury

In the weeks leading up to July 1789, the *Mercury*'s columns were full of reports from France which, after several disastrous harvests, decades of social unrest and a century of political theorising, was clearly on the verge of cataclysmic change. In May the Estates General, the body comprising representatives of the clergy, the nobility and the rising middle classes, (largely lawyers and bureaucrats), were summoned by the King, Louis XVI, and his minister, Necker, to meet at Versailles to debate the financial problems of the nation.

There were weeks of argument about procedure: whether the votes in the Estates General should be counted individually or as blocks from each of the three Estates. Eventually, in June, the Third Estate, joined by a small number of the clergy and indeed led by one of them, the Abbé Sieyès, voted to declare themselves the National Assembly without reference to the other two Estates. Locked out of their meeting rooms at Versailles, the deputies from the Third Estate met in a nearby 'real tennis' court and swore an oath not to disperse until: *the constitution of the realm and public regeneration are established and assured.* After huge public unrest, and attempts by Necker and the King to defuse the situation, all the members of the Nobility and Clergy were finally ordered by the King, Louis XVI, to join the Third Estate in the National Assembly.

The Tennis Court Oath
Jacques-Louis David, *The Tennis Court Oath* (1791), Musée National du Château, Versailles

It looked as if constitutional change had been achieved peacefully and the *Mercury's* correspondent wrote hopefully, on the 13th of July, the very eve of the outbreak of revolution, that *everything is to be expected from the patriotic enthusiasm of the people.*

The following edition, however, reported the storming of the Bastille, after days of increasingly violent attacks on public officials. Even at this point the Reading paper seemed inclined to take an optimistic view of events. The report on the Bastille emphasised the sorry state of the prisoners and the joy of the people at their release. A later issue would report that during the demolition of the citadel an iron cage containing a human skeleton had been found in a deep dungeon at the prison.

The following day the army, which had been encircling Paris, withdrew and, according to the *Mercury* of the 20th of July: *It was currently reported that a considerable part of Paris had been destroyed by fire...The University is levelled to the ground.* The article continues by stating that *the fear of famine is more formidable than ever.*

By the next issue, the tone is again more hopeful: *We are happy to say that the excesses have been magnified. The Archbishop of Paris was not assassinated.* Moreover, *A grand Te Deum* (the great Catholic hymn of thanksgiving) *for the deliverance of the nation from despotism was sung the 16th in the church of Notre Dame.*

As a weekly newspaper, the *Mercury* must have found it very difficult to keep up with the pace of events in France. The mood swings between optimism and alarm. It is clear that rumours had been multiplying about the scale of disorder in Paris. This was partly because refugees, frightened by events in France, were already starting to arrive in England. The article goes on: *The number of French families, whom the present commotions in their own country have forced to take refuge in this, are almost incredible.*

Gradually the reports from France in the *Mercury* become more sensational. In late July the paper carried the information that in Soissons, near Rheims, a mob had attacked and decapitated two people accused of hoarding corn. Riots were breaking out all over the country. Rouen was reported to be *most dreadfully convulsed* and there had been *great violence* in Strasbourg. In mid-August the paper printed a story about an outrage in Mans-en-Maine where a group of peasants, asked by the lord of the manor to cut grass for his own use, had *inhumanely set on him and chopped off his head.* The same fate had befallen the mayor of St. Denis, who had been accused of embezzling corn. It is very striking how many of these incidents involve bread or corn. Food, as much as liberty, seems to have been the driving force of the tumult. As is well known, several years of bad harvests, linked to volcanic eruptions thousands of miles from Europe, played a major part in the events of 1789 and their aftermath. The paper reported that when the canons of a church refused to distribute a quarter of their tithes to the local poor people, a custom which had fallen into disuse, they were besieged first by 400 and later by 1000 women who forced the local official to distribute 15,000 pounds of grain.

It appears that some of the perpetrators of these attacks were claiming royal approval for their actions, as, on the 24th of August, the *Mercury* reported that the King had issued a royal proclamation denying *claims by bands of robbers that the king approves of attacks on castles, carrying off of records and other outrages to property.* Such disorders were, according to the King, *a scandal and a disgrace to France.* However, as the paper had already reported in late July, the power of the King was *daily abating*, and much worse was to follow, as subsequent events would make clear.

Some moves by the new National Assembly met with the *Mercury*'s approbation. In mid September the paper reported approvingly that the delegates were *modelling the constitution* which they were *every day bringing nearer to the English model*, and two months later the readers learned that a version of Habeas Corpus had been approved, by which *it shall not be lawful for the officers of police to imprison any person by way of correction for more than three days without bringing him to trial.*

The Revolution and the Church

However, the issue which caused the greatest disquiet to the proprietors of the paper, and which was to have a significant effect on Reading, as on the rest of England, was the question of the rights and duties of the clergy.

One of the first acts of the new Assembly had been to set up a committee for ecclesiastical reform, with the intention of revitalising the French Church, bringing it into harmony with Revolutionary principles and providing a secure financial basis for its work. Many priests saw this as an opportunity to return to the discipline of the early Church. It should be remembered that some of the foremost personalities of the Revolution were themselves members of the clergy. These included the Abbé Sieyès, author of the pamphlet, *What is the Third Estate?* and Talleyrand, the Bishop of Autun. The latter would end the Revolution as one of Napoleon's three consuls and his boast when he was asked in later life, *What did you do during the Revolution?* was, *I survived.*

By the *Renunciations* of the 4th of August 1789, the French bishops were deprived of all feudal dues and parish priests lost tithes and vestry fees. The *Mercury* reported, on the 24th of August, that: *The Clergy, to their credit, have given up their right to tithes and thrown themselves entirely on the mercy of the people with whom they have agreed to pay an equal quota in all taxes to be levied for the use of the public.* Soon afterwards the *Annates,* benefices paid to the Pope, were abolished and, in September of that year, the Papal territories of Avignon were annexed to France. Preparations were also set in train for the closure of all religious houses and February 1790 was to see the dissolution of the religious orders in France. All monasteries and convents were to be closed unless they were involved in educational or charitable work. Effectively this meant the end of the contemplative orders, a move which was not entirely unpopular among the secular clergy, some of whom regarded the contemplatives as *useless parasites.*

In early September, 1789, the *Mercury* included the news that the Benedictine nuns of St. Fargan had written to the National Assembly, praying *that their house may not be included in the general suppression of such establishments.*

No doubt hundreds of such pleas were received by the Assembly, but to no avail. In November the *Mercury* reported that the National Assembly had formally decreed that: *All ecclesiastical property is at the disposal of the Nation* and that *no vows whatever shall be made in future in any monastery.*

Louis, despite grave misgivings, reluctantly signed the decree.

A contemporary cartoon depicts nuns and monks rejoicing in their new freedom. The caption in translation reads: *What a happy day this is for us, sisters. The title of mother and wife is so much better than that of nun.*

However, as a letter published by the *Mercury* on the 22nd of October bears witness, the reality was very different. The letter, to *Miss S****,* (presumably Smart), from a nun in Boulogne, almost certainly a former schoolfriend of Marianne and Elizabeth who had become the Reverend Mother of the convent, vividly depicts the sufferings undergone by many religious:

Since I had the pleasure of seeing you, my dear friend, we have weathered a most dreadful storm. By the first of October the nuns were all to leave their convents. The Annunciades and Ursulines of this place are now dispersed in the town, separated from each other, stript of everything, and hopeless of the pensions which had been promised them. I was not deceived. I foresaw that having seized all our possessions, sold everything they could move of our property, we should be left without resource. They are now selling off the Ursulines; they tear up the very boards: they tell me it is deplorable to see the confusion that reigns in that dear house, that was always so neat and orderly. What a sacrifice.

On the 29th of September, there came Commissioners to demand the altar plate, and whatever there was of value in the service of the church. I was obliged to appear; I never suffered so cruelly; nature shudders at the remembrance. We are without altars, without ministers, without the least spiritual consolation; separated from our sisters, we are divided into six different societies, one of eight, the others of six each, and three are gone to their families. I cannot describe to you the grief of all, when the hour of parting came. Every one, their eyes bathed in tears, surveyed the rest in silence, unable to utter a word. The first division went out on the Thursday at two o'clock in the morning, a second on the Friday at seven o'clock in the evening, the third and fourth in the night of Friday, and the fifth and last in the night between Saturday and Sunday. What a sad spectacle! It is impossible to describe it – it must have been seen – I leave you to judge of it. The holy place in every way profaned. – Pity your poor friend, doomed to close the door of her asylum against herself, and to deliver up the keys to an officer of the district.

I endured as many agonies as there were Nuns to separate, all of whom testified the most tender and sincere attachment. Bred up in this convent from two years old, I never passed but one night out of it, and that against my will. I am consumed with grief: ten days have appeared to me as ten years; if God does not support me, I must sink. The pillage of our convent is deplorable; they tear it piece-meal and sell it by lathes and boards. I requested the wood which we had laid in for winter store, and paid for it; it was denied me; and, having been promised a quarter in advance, we are told that we are to receive nothing till January. Yet we must subsist, have fire, candles, buy secular habits, as we are not permitted to wear our own, and where are the means? Where is charity? Yet we must rejoice in God, since it is his will we should be thus destitute.

The nobility are great sufferers; the brother in law of your friend loses, at a stroke, more than one hundred thousand livres, by the deprivation of his rights. Taxes are very high; great and small complain; every one is aggrieved; wrongs multiply; and do you ask the reason you are answered it is the law. Yet we must not lose our patience, nor our hope, and heaven will comfort us. – This is our state at present, yet do not afflict yourself, my dear friend; pray to God for the poor outcasts – his help is most necessary to us. I write with a wandering mind, you will not be surprised, and excuse me; when I get a little composure I may be more connected, perhaps at present my eyes dim and my head giddy; every day it seems to me as if what had passed the day before was a dream.

The effect on the monastic buildings of France was catastrophic. Some abbeys were saved, as in England during the Reformation, by becoming parish churches. Others, such as the Abbey of Jumièges in Normandy, shown below, were appropriated by the State and sold off, often to be used as quarries. Ironically the abbot of Jumièges had refused to allow his abbey to become the parish church as he considered it too grand for such a purpose.

Ruins of Jumièges Abbey

The English poet, Wordsworth, initially a great supporter of the Revolution, visited France in 1790 and was shocked to see the Grande Chartreuse monastery lying empty after the expulsion of the monks. In *The Prelude* he imagines Nature crying: *Stay, stay your sacrilegious hands.* His disenchantment with Revolutionary ideology arguably began with this experience.

The Civil Constitution of the Clergy

Under the *Civil Constitution of the Clergy*, a law prepared by the Committee for Ecclesiastical Reform, the whole structure of the French Church was revised. The old dioceses of France were abolished and replaced with fewer new ones, each corresponding to a *département*, or civil administrative area.

All clergy became salaried state employees and were to be elected by the laity of their parishes, whether Catholic or not. There was to be no contact with foreign bishops, thus severely limiting the powers of the Papacy. The Pope himself, unsure how to react, hesitated before issuing his answer to these moves and in the meantime Louis signed the measures into law. Between September and December 1790 all clergy were required to swear the *Serment constitutionnel*, or Constitutional Oath, pledging allegiance to the Nation, the King and the Law. This oath had to be taken in public, after High Mass, outside each church. Some priests took the oath, believing that they should stay with their congregations even if this meant compromising their principles. In the end roughly half the French clergy refused to sign.

In April 1791 the Pope, in his letter *Caritas,* rejected the Civil Constitution of the Clergy. By November of that year the Legislative Assembly had declared all 'non-juring' priests to be 'suspect' and liable to deportation from their communes. A year later, in March 1792, all such priests were given two weeks to leave the country or face deportation to France's notoriously unhealthy penal colony of Guiana, in South America.

Emigration from France had already reached extraordinary levels. As early as August 1789 the *Mercury* had reported that *numbers are every day emigrating and the packet boats from Dieppe and Calais are perpetually crowded with French passengers.*

By October it was obvious that it was not only clergy and nobles who were leaving: *No man of property or of sense who can possibly get away, will remain there, even industrious mechanics and ingenious artists...will seek bread in England.*

War and the Execution of the King, 1792 - 1793

France went to war with Austria and Prussia in the spring of 1792. By August that year the Prussian armies were advancing into France and panic broke out as Revolutionaries searched for possible subversives. A rumour that prisoners in Parisian jails were being armed by Royalists led to several murderous attacks on prisons. One of these was at the *Carmes*, a former Carmelite monastery in Paris, which was being used to house large numbers of suspect priests while they awaited trial. A mob broke into the prison and the priests were herded into the garden where they were either shot or hacked to death.

The Massacre of Les Carmes

Those who attempted to take refuge in the chapel were hauled out and killed. Only a few escaped. One of these 'Martyrs of the Carmes' was Louis Longuet, whose brother François was to play an important part in Reading's Catholic history. The martyrs were beatified in 1926.

The columns of the *Mercury* in late 1792 and the beginning of 1793 are full of accounts of the trial of Louis XVI. On the 15th of October the paper carried the report from the *Convention*, as the legislative body of France was now called, declaring:

1. *That every charge relative to the king is proved.*
2. *That no charge relative to the venality of the Legislative Assembly is substantiated*
3. *That there is full evidence that many of the unfortunate men imprisoned by the committee and butchered during the late riots were most excellent patriots.*

This last declaration can have been of little comfort to relatives of the Carmes martyrs.

At the end of October the Reading paper reported that: *The King bears the loss of his crown with a manly composure and is prepared for death.*

The edition of the *Mercury* published on the 23rd of January 1793, makes sombre reading. The front page contains the voting figures concerning the death sentence passed on the King, with 319 members of the Convention voting for banishment but the majority, of 366, demanding *death without restriction*. Despite pleas from his defence counsel that the sentence be suspended, the decree of execution was passed.

Page two of the paper carries an account of Louis' execution. It begins: *The unfortunate Louis XVI is no more. He was beheaded yesterday morning at 10 o'clock in the Place de Louis XV. He died with the most heroic fortitude.*

The *Mercury* reported the King's last words, which indicate how bitterly he regretted having signed the anti-clerical laws: *I recommend my soul to God. I pardon my enemies. I die innocent. I only sanctioned upon compulsion the Civil Constitution of the Clergy.*

The article states that *further words were drowned by drums*. It goes on to quote extracts from Louis' Will in which he asked pardon of God for having sanctioned the decree of the Civil Constitution of the Clergy, *although this sanction was extorted by violence and was contrary to his solemn protest*. In his Will the King acknowledged that he had freely accepted all other parts of the Constitution. A long obituary of the King ends with the prophetic words: *Unquestionably the blood of the unfortunate monarch will invite vengeance on his murderers.*

CHAPTER 2

The Exodus of the Clergy

England and the Emigré Clergy

These horrific events, and particularly the king's execution, led to a mass exodus of French clergy. They went not just to England but to countries all over Europe, normally according to whichever frontier was nearest: the Low Countries, Italy, Spain, Portugal, Germany, even Russia, Many went to French-speaking Canada, British territory since the Seven Years' War, to found religious communities there. A report in the *Mercury* dated 31st December 1792 notes that on the previous Monday: *Several of the heads of the French refugee clergy were admitted to an interview with Mr Pitt* for a conference on settling many of them in Canada.

Geography meant that most of the refugees coming to England were from Northern and Western France. A report dated 29th October 1792 stated: *The number of French refugees that have arrived in England to the 13th instant is 6881, in Jersey and Guernsey 3000, total 9881, of which three fourths are computed to be priests.*

Nuns, too, were taking refuge in England. The same issue of the paper reported that: *Last Wednesday were landed at Black Rock, near Shoreham, from the Prince of Wales' packet, Captain Burton*, (sic) *37 nuns. They were all from one convent and most of them elderly ladies.*

The following edition carried the extra information that these nuns were from a convent in Lille and that they had been visited by the Prince of Wales and Mrs Fitzerbert, with whom the future King George IV had entered into a form of marriage (illegal because not approved by the King), in 1785. It is significant that she was a Catholic. It was also reported that the Prince had set up a subscription for them.

Most of the émigré French clergy who came to England were Normans or Bretons. Bellenger, the author of the authoritative work *The French Exiled Clergy,* states that in September 1792 there were already one and a half thousand French priests in England, a figure which had risen by December of that year to between six and seven thousand. Initially about half of these priests took refuge in the Channel Islands but later events forced most of these to move to mainland Britain.

As the Revolutionary armies moved across Europe fresh waves of emigrants arrived and any attempted Royalist revolt in France brought further repression and even more arrivals from across the Channel. Some priests were even rescued from ships taking them to Guiana when these craft were intercepted by British warships.

Reactions to the Arrival of the Exiled French Clergy 1792 – 1796

Emigrant clergy © The Trustees of the British Museum

The caption to this Cruikshank cartoon reads, *Emigrant clergy reading the late Decree that all who returns* (sic) *shall be put to Death*. This confirms a report from the *Mercury*, at the end of November 1792, of a decree that *all emigrants who returned to France should quit France on pain of death*.

As was to be expected, reactions in England varied widely to this influx of Catholic clergy, from a country with which Great Britain was at war. Many people, including a large number of Anglican clergymen, were sympathetic. Oxford University printed large numbers of Catholic bibles especially for them.

However certain sections of the population, as might be expected, exhibited anti-French sentiment. An article in the *Gentleman's Magazine* described the priests as *locusts swarming over our English fields*. There were those who argued that 'Charity begins at home', with the deserving English poor. There was also a good deal of anti-Papist propaganda, especially in some parts of the country, including Oxfordshire.

The *Mercury,* along with newspapers elsewhere in the country, printed the following report on the 15th of October, 1792, relating to a private subscription fund to support the emigrant clergy:

At a meeting held in the Guildhall, in the city of Winchester ... It was unanimously resolved:
First: That the Subscriptions already received should be retained by the respective bankers, till the same are directed to be disposed of by the Subscribers who are hereby requested to signify to the bankers to which Committee in London their several Subscriptions are to be transmitted.

Secondly That the money which shall, in future, be subscribed, be considered as for the benefit of the French Clergy only, and that the same be accordingly transmitted (once a fortnight), by the bankers, with the names of the subscribers, to the Committee at the Free Man's Tavern in London.

A later edition contained a list of banks into which subscriptions could be paid. These were in Winchester, Southampton, Portsmouth, Gosport, Basingstoke, Newport in the Isle of Wight, Andover, Ringwood and Lymington. This indicates that most of the refugees were, as might be expected, concentrated in the seaports of Southern England. There is no mention of Reading in the list, though it would not be long before French priests appeared in the town, as described in Chapter 3, below.

A memoir published many decades afterwards, in an 1881 edition of *The Dublin Review*, the Catholic magazine founded in 1836 by Cardinal Wiseman and Daniel O'Connell, indicates the sort of anti-Catholic sentiment which may have greeted the first priests to come to Reading. It tells of a newly arrived émigré cleric who was thrown into the Thames by three young fanatics who recognised him as a Papist. The highly emotional account tells of how *this latter-day Saint Stephen*, before sinking beneath the waters, piously raised his arms to heaven, praying that his persecutors would not die until their eyes had been opened to the light of truth. The narrator tells us that two of the perpetrators died soon afterwards but the third, on his deathbed, to the astonishment of his family, asked for a Catholic priest, confessed his crime and was received into the Church.

In 1792 the Emigrant Relief Committee suggested allocating a large public building to house emigrant clergy. It was decided, possibly at the suggestion of the Marquis of Buckingham, whose wife was a Catholic, to use the King's House, Winchester. Next to Winchester Castle, this had been built for Charles II to a design by Christopher Wren. Planned as the English Versailles, it had been allowed to fall into disrepair during the eighteenth century when it was used to house French prisoners, who were forced to sleep in hammocks because the floors were rotten. Some windows were glassless and many doors had been ripped out. An estimate was given that it would cost £500 and take five weeks work to fit out the south wing for 500 clergy.

George III, who seems to have been sympathetic to the French exiles, particularly following Louis XVI's execution, gave permission for the house to be used but asked that 'attentive persons' should be kept in the house to detect any suspicious activity.

In autumn 1792 the first priests arrived and by February of the following year 221 of them were installed in *airy comfortable rooms* with bedding provided, after some persuasion, by local hospitals. It was envisaged that around 650 priests would live at the King's House but, by the time it closed in early 1796, there seem to have been over a thousand in residence.

The King's House, Winchester (Courtesy of Winchester Museum)

Coloured lithograph. 'View from the Airing Ground Sketched During Festivities held to Celebrate the Coronation of Queen Victoria' by Richard Baigent and printed by C. Hullmandel. 1838.

The house was run along the lines of a French seminary and was headed by the Abbé Paul Thomas Martin, a member of the Eudist congregation of priests who specialised in training candidates for the priesthood.

In 1793 the 'King's Letter' made a national appeal for funds to support these priests. It was read in all Anglican churches and Catholic chapels on various Sundays between mid April and the beginning of November. Many Dissenters' chapels agreed to read the letter, although some dissenting Ministers accused the Church of England of consorting with the *Great Harlot,* and one writer felt that *Atheism with all its horrors* was *preferable to Popery.*

Despite these reservations by some groups, a total of £41,314. 2s. 7d was raised, four times the expected amount.

Those priests capable of supporting themselves were expected to do so. At Winchester a number worked in a tapestry manufactory set up by the Marchioness of Buckingham. Others were employed as tutors in schools or private houses.

The priests left a memorial of their stay in the vestibule of their chapel in Winchester. It is a marble tablet, inscribed in Latin, and paid for by the Marquis of Buckingham, after the priests expressed their wish to provide a lasting symbol of their gratitude, but lamented that they had no money to buy one. The Marquis expressly gave instructions that his name was not to appear among the list of benefactors. The tablet, and an English translation, are today in the Church of St. Peter in Winchester.

The King's House itself was gutted by fire in 1894 and was demolished. Some of its columns and masonry can still be seen in the Peninsula Barracks which replaced it in 1900.

Peninsula Barracks, Winchester.

As early as November 1793, rumours had begun to circulate that the house would be needed as military barracks. Since alternative accommodation would be required, newspaper advertisements started to appear asking for 'mansion houses' as lodgings for French priests.

Although the Prime Minister, Pitt, originally had no intention of going to war against Revolutionary France, the King's execution and the French army's invasion of the Low Countries, plus the threat of revolution in England itself, changed government policy, and Britain began to mobilise for war.

CHAPTER 3

The French Priests in Reading, 1796 – 1802

Arrival in Reading

As we have seen, a small group of French priests had already arrived in Reading and were, by 1792, living in Finch's Buildings. Probably the fact that they had been accepted, without serious objections, by the townspeople, contributed to the choice of Reading as a suitable place of residence for the Winchester refugees. It was also sufficiently far from the coast to dispel fears of some émigrés acting as spies in naval dockyards.

In August 1796 the Winchester community was broken up, with just 150 clergy remaining there. It appears that the priests were dispersed gradually, to avoid giving the impression of large numbers of Frenchmen travelling through the country and possibly triggering an invasion scare. About 100 Bretons went to a large house in Thame, while forty of the Normans settled in Paddington, then a village outside London. However the majority, mostly from Normandy, came to Reading, to the King's Arms Hotel in Castle Street (now Castle Hill), an old coaching inn originating in the reign of Charles I, which was requisitioned by the British government.

Castle Hill House Today

Life in the Reading House

The Abbé Martin came from Winchester to be the superior of the Reading House, as it was generally known. Numbers grew rapidly, from 25 in September 1796 to 189 in November and 200 by the end of the year. We have detailed information on these numbers because a monthly list had to be supplied to the Government in order to obtain 'sustentation funds' for those priests unable to support themselves. A list dating from the end of the century, now in the Public Record Office, names 342 priests.

Image from Plasse: Le clergé émigré français

The above engraving was one of a pair, the second showing the Winchester house, presented to the Blount family at Mapledurham by Father Charles Lefèbvre, one of the exiled priests. He was employed by the Blounts as an archivist to work on their family history. The engravings were later given, by the Blounts, to the French Chapel in King's Street, London.

There are considerable differences between the house in the engraving and the present-day building on Castle Hill. Today we see a curved bay on the left wing of the house, a plain frontage and a large cedar of Lebanon in the front garden. The engraving shows us a flat left wing, a colonnaded frontage giving the impression almost of a cloister, and a parterre of flowerbeds. These were obviously designed to convey the priests' gratitude to their hosts and particularly King George.

The central bed reads, *GR. God save the King.* The remaining beds are planted with heart or star shapes surrounded by inscriptions, worked in flowers or stones. Around the stars are the messages, *Blest star our guide,* in English, and *You could not have guided us better,* in French. The right hand star is surrounded by the Latin inscription, *He always loves those who love him.* Most significantly, around the left hand star, are the English words, *Rooted by gratitude.* It seems very likely that the magnificent Cedar of Lebanon we see today was planted as a sapling by the French priests. Estimates of its age by Reading Council would seem to support this theory but a dendrochronological sample might confirm it.

The priests' routine was similar to that followed in Winchester, with Masses beginning at 5 am and Divine Office at the appointed times throughout the day. According to Eppstein's *History of the Faith in an English Town* they *led a monastic life, only leaving their cloister for a daily ramble in the then quiet and rural glades in their vicinity.* High Mass was celebrated on Sundays and there was daily Benediction in the chapel which, it has been claimed, could hold 400 worshippers. It was probably the former ballroom of the hotel. The author of the Cowslade Manuscript, probably Eleanora Cowslade, Marianne's daughter, wrote her recollections of the chapel:

Memory can still take me back to my first attendance at the service in the King's Arms, where, from my seat I watched the priests as they entered the Chapel, each with a book in his hand and a low wooden stool under his arm. One of them ascended the pulpit and gave the signal of preparation by a sonorous blow of his nose, thus awakening a chorus long and loud which was renewed at certain pauses in the sermon, the preacher each time giving the note to this, to me, extraordinary performance.

After the sermon Benediction was given from the Altar which, with its wax tapers, the real labour of the bees, and profusion of flowers (justly called artificial) presented to me a grand spectacle, and I remember a feeling of surprise on being commended as a good little girl for having been quiet and orderly during the long service.

The house was certainly not big enough to accommodate all the priests. In November 1797 the list states that 231 priests were living in the house and a further 104 in lodgings in the town. The original four priests who had been welcomed by the Smart family continued to live in Finch's buildings. The locals must have become used to seeing the priests make their way to the House for services, each carrying a breviary and a low 'chapel stool' on which to sit.

As in Winchester some priests earned their own keep while others, especially the sick and infirm, relied on the sustentation funds provided by the Government.

Further evidence of the priests' gratitude is afforded by a book of poems entitled *Pièces de poésie,* written by a priest called N. Leguay. Curiously, this name does not appear on any of the lists of priests in Scantlebury or Bellenger. The book is dedicated to Louis XVIII, who became the King of France in exile, after the death of his nephew, Louis XVII, in prison. This would indicate that the book was published after 1795. The collection includes a remarkable *Letter of thanks to the English nation, and particularly the people of Reading,* (see Appendix A). Note the slightly unconvincing descriptions of the environs of Reading and the very fulsome eulogy of George III as well as the damning verdict on the Revolution. The writer is clearly a monarchist and bitterly opposed to all political innovation.

Another token of gratitude is the engraved box held in Reading Museum, which has on its lid what is clearly a copy of the engraving given by Father Lefèbvre. It also has two views of the Abbey gateway and a picture of the King's House in Winchester. The sides of the box show what is described as a rear view of the house and a picture of *Mr Blount's house at Mapledurham.*

The interior of the lid holds a detailed description, in French, of these images plus an interesting detail: the picture on the lid is not an exact representation as several large trees which block the view of the house have been omitted. There is no indication of where these trees were or of how they relate to the flowerbeds.

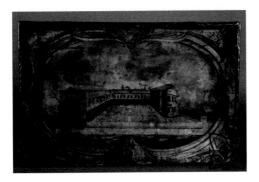

The French Priests' Box - Photograph courtesy of Reading Museum

We only have tantalising glimpses of how the priests lived in Reading. An equal mystery attaches to their deaths and burial. According to a document held in the National Archives, with a copy in Bayeux, the priests who died in Reading were buried in Cumberland Road in East Reading. However this road did not exist at the turn of the nineteenth century, being part of a Victorian development begun in the 1860's. An appendix to Scantlebury's *The Catholic Registers of Reading*, contributed by Cyril Weale, began to unravel the mystery. It contains a register of the burials of French priests and other French émigrés in Winchester and thereabouts. The first entry for the Reading clergy includes mention of the new cemetery given over for the burial of French priests who had lived in the house given to these clergy in the town of Reading, situated 'near to the said house' *(près ladite maison).*

Newspaper articles published in the 20th century indicate that the burial plot may have been at the bottom of the orchard behind the house, and some of these reports suggest that the graves were still there when the articles were written. However part of this land was sold off for housing in Victorian times and more in the 1970's, so if the burials still remain they are now beneath houses, flats or gardens. The garden of the house itself is today very small.

A possible alternative scenario emerged during a visit to the Portsmouth diocesan archives. A document indicated that the cemetery could have been closed when the priests returned to France. If so the remains may have been disinterred and possibly taken to the larger French graveyard in Winchester. However evidence from the Winchester archives indicates that this cemetery was obliterated by the digging of a cutting when the railway came to the city in 1840.

The cemetery record gives few details of individual deaths other than the ages of the priests and their original parishes. Several of the priests seem to have died young, possibly of cholera. Some further details emerge from occasional newspaper reports. The *Reading Mercury* of August the 20th 1798 carried the tragic story of a priest found drowned in the millstream near Caversham lock: *He had been angling, and his line, as is supposed, hitching in the weeds, he undressed himself all but his shirt and went into the water to get it out. When found, he was near the shore and had the bough of a tree fast clenched in his hand. He had left his clothes in the lock-shutter's boat, and in his pocket were three small fishes.*

An entry in the burial registers of St. Peter's Church, Caversham, strongly suggests that this was Pierre Nourry (his name is given as 'Peter Nourry, an emigrant'), who came from the diocese of Coutances.

Return to France, 1802

In November 1799, following his coup of the 18th Brumaire, Napoleon came to power as First Consul, putting an end to the Revolution and paving the way for the First Empire.

In August that same year Pius VI had died in exile in France. As Rome was occupied by French troops, the Conclave to elect his successor was held in Venice. The new Pope was a Benedictine, Chiaramonti, the Bishop of Imola, who took the name Pius VII. He had already excited some controversy by his Christmas sermon in 1797, declaring that Christianity was not necessarily incompatible with democracy and that *equality is not an idea of philosophers but of Christ.*

Napoleon's own attitude to religion was strictly pragmatic. A non-believer himself, he nonetheless saw religion as an essential tool of an ordered society, stating that: *No society can exist without morality; no good morality without religion.* It was claimed that during his Egyptian campaign he let it be believed that he had converted to Islam to endear himself to the Egyptian people.

When Pitt, Napoleon's arch-enemy, left office in March 1801, the new Prime Minister, Addington, began peace negotiations. The Peace of Amiens was signed, to great rejoicing, in March 1802. The peace had been preceded by a Concordat between the French State and the Church, and a solemn Mass was celebrated in Notre Dame on Easter Day 1802 to mark the resurrection of the Church in France. Though the Concordat restored the free exercise of the Faith, it did not mark a return to the pre-Revolutionary French church. Bishops were appointed by the state and all clergy remained state employees who were to swear allegiance to the state in all but spiritual matters. One Italian cardinal described the French Church as *the shadow of a religion being re-established.*

The way was clear for the émigré priests in England to return to France. Most of them did so but a few remained in England, some clearly because they had established themselves within the local Catholic community, some out of political conviction. A significant minority of the émigré clergy in England were deeply opposed to Pius VII's policy of collaboration with Napoleon and acceptance of democracy. Their leader was Pierre Louis Blanchard and they were known as Blanchardists. Fiercely monarchist and traditionalist, these clerics saw Pius VII as a traitor to the Church and even as a heretic. Blanchard was reported as having stated:

To save his faith Pius VI lost his throne.
To save his throne Pius VII abandoned his faith.

The Vicars Apostolic, the Bishops appointed by Rome to administer the Catholic Church in England, agonised over how to cope with this threatened schism within its ranks. Eventually, in 1818, it was announced that all French clergy remaining in England should sign an oath asserting the supremacy of the Pope and agreeing to teach this to others. We know that of the priests remaining in Reading at least two refused to sign, their names being given as Le Tellier and Le Noge (possibly La Noë). One of Bishop Poynter's Vicars General, the Rev. Mr Hodgson, reported in a letter that both Lefèbvre and La Blardière had signed. What we cannot know, though we may hazard a guess, is the attitude of the French priest who was to have the greatest influence on the lives of Reading's Catholic population.

SECTION B

REBIRTH

PART 1

The Life of François Longuet

and

His Work in Reading

CHAPTER 1

The Young François Longuet

The Early Life of François Longuet

We know far more about François Longuet than any of the other French priests. Ironically, and sadly, this is because his work in Reading was brought to such a tragic end. Much of our information about this interesting, and in many ways attractive, character, comes from documents written after his untimely death.

François was the youngest of ten children of Nicolas Longuet and Madeleine de Boucq. His father was a prosperous farmer in the diocese of Séez in Normandy. François was born in 1771. We know little about his early life but his brother Louis, 14 years his senior, went into a seminary when François was only 6 and was ordained in 1881 when François was 10 years old.

François was 18 when the Revolution broke out. By then his brother Louis was a curate in the local diocese and belonged to the Chapter of Tours cathedral. Although he was not required to take the oath because he was not a parish priest, Louis opposed the new order and went into hiding. He was arrested in August 1792 and imprisoned in the Carmes prison in Paris where he was murdered by the Revolutionary mob which broke into the prison. François was then 21.

We have a picture of François which shows him as a handsome young man with a hairstyle very typical of the Revolutionary period. It is a sketch, reproduced in Scantlebury's book, *The Catholic Registers of Reading,* published in the 1920s, and is a copy from the original portrait kept by the Longuet family in France. A note under the drawing states that it is a *crayon* (pencil) *drawing by Mme Desprairies of Bayeux* based on this oil painting. Sadly neither the original nor the sketch can now be traced.

François probably arrived in England in 1792 or 1793. At this stage he was not ordained but had received the tonsure and was in minor orders in the seminary in Caen, where he was studying philosophy. His parents, following the death of his brother Louis, may have urged him to go to England or he may have made the decision himself after the execution of the King at the beginning of 1793. We know that he was strongly royalist: his ring was engraved with the motto *Pro Deo et Rege* (For God and the King) and the French coat of arms. Records show that he lodged in Portsmouth with a widow called Mrs Childe. At some point after arriving in England he was ordained but he does not feature in the lists of émigré priests receiving financial help from the British Government. This was probably because he was able to support himself by teaching French and Latin. Soon after coming to England he will have received news of the death of his father. Other than that we know nothing of his movements for nearly ten years.

First Years in Reading, 1802 – 1808.

François Longuet was definitely in Reading by 1802. The Reading Mission records show that he officiated at a baptism in October of that year. By this time most of the French priests in Reading had returned to France and the Castle Hill house had been closed. Finch's Buildings was home to those priests who were still opposed to the new Concordat in France or who had decided to stay to minister to the Catholic community in Reading. Some, such as the Abbé Godquin, had limited English, just enough to hear confessions and attend sick parishioners. It might be expected that they would welcome this young, energetic priest with open arms.

In fact relations appear to have become strained for reasons which cannot be known, although it is possible that they regarded him as 'too English' and not sufficiently identified with their old way of doing things.

We know, for example, that by 1809 Longuet was using the Roman Breviary like his English colleagues, to the great approval of his superior in the English Mission, Bishop William Poynter, the assistant to John Douglass, Vicar Apostolic for the London area. The Finch's Buildings priests, like the majority of the French émigré clergy, would have used the Gallican breviary. Having been ordained in England, Longuet may have been trained to do things the English way, which to the Finch's Buildings priests must have felt like 'going native' as a later generation would say in the British empire. However, his name does not appear in the lists of students at St. Edmund's College, Ware, and it has been suggested that he completed his studies and was ordained at the King's House in Winchester.

A letter from Mr (we would now call him Father), Webster, the priest at Woolhampton, to Bishop Poynter in March 1817, after Longuet's death, gives us an interesting picture of how the Catholic community in Reading was served by both local and French clergy verbose and his use of punctuation sparse. However it is worth struggling through his long sentences to get a hint of annoyance at the young priest 'muscling in' on his territory:

You are well aware, I presume, of the manner in which the Catholics of Reading have been attended since Sir H. Englefield's family at Whiteknights, not far from it, left the county, viz. by the Missionary at Ufton Court about 8 miles distant who went to them chiefly at Indulgences to what is now called the Old Chapel, receiving from Sir Henry £20 per annum now reduced to £10. As far, therefore as the remaining congregation at Ufton Court and neighbourhood sought and received spiritual succour from the Woolhampton mission after the death of its pastor, the late Mr. Baynham, I felt myself called upon to extend my humble service to the other seeming part of it at Reading, till Mr. Longuet sought for and obtained its general superintendence.

The 'Old Chapel' referred to must be Finch's Buildings. It is not clear from the letter when exactly François *sought for and obtained* the superintendence of the Reading mission. He would have had to apply to the then Vicar Apostolic of the London District, Bishop John Douglass, who had been appointed to this role in 1790, a year before the Catholic Relief Act.

Evidence indicates that, by 1808, Longuet had decided to found a new chapel with its own presbytery, both to assert his independence from Finch's Buildings and to accommodate Reading's expanding Catholic population.

Bishop John Douglass,
Vicar Apostolic of London District, 1790 - 1812

Bishop William Poynter,
Coadjutor to Bishop Douglass 1803 -1812,
Vicar Apostolic of the London District, 1812 -1827

Portraits of Bishops Poynter and Douglass courtesy of St Edmund's College, Ware.

CHAPTER 2

The Longuet - Poynter Correspondence and Plans for a Chapel

Proposals for a New Chapel

A collection of letters preserved in the Westminster diocesan archives sheds some light on the sequence of events leading up to the establishment of Longuet's new chapel. The letters are mostly to Longuet from Bishop William Poynter, who was Douglass' Coadjutor Bishop before succeeding him in 1812, after Douglass' death. Before this date Poynter was President of the newly founded St Edmund's College at Old Hall Green, Ware, in Hertfordshire.

Poynter had been educated at Douai, where he had become Director of Studies at the English College, prior to its enforced closure during the Revolution. During the disturbances following the King's execution, drunken soldiers demanded entry to the college, although it was in theory exempt from Revolutionary decrees. Poynter confronted them, and a group of the students allowed themselves to be carried through the streets shouting 'Vive la nation! Vive la liberté!', thus saving their colleagues from the mob. Later he was imprisoned in the castle at Doullens, with his students, and became famous for reciting the Divine Office on the ramparts separating the two citadels in which the seminarians were imprisoned.

The sequence of letters starts in January 1809 with Poynter promising Longuet that he will speak to the Vicar Apostolic about *the subject of your Chapel.* This would suggest that the young priest had made the suggestion late in 1808. A clue as to the possible impetus for this comes from a later letter, sent to Poynter in April 1811, by Mrs Smart's two daughters, Marianne Cowslade and Elizabeth Lenoir. They were angry with Longuet because he wanted to transfer the chapel furniture from Finch's Buildings to his new chapel. This furniture had originally come from Sir Henry Englefield's mansion at Whiteknights. The dispute had obviously become acrimonious and the sisters sent Bishop Poynter a copy of the letter Longuet had written to them about the matter. In their own letter to the Bishop, Marianne and Elizabeth refer to Longuet having been asked to leave his apartment *in our house* (presumably Finch's Buildings) by Mrs Smart, *in consequence of repeated complaints against him for a conduct which gave scandal and much uneasiness to the Clergymen residing with him.*

We have no means of knowing what behaviour this refers to, and it would be unfair to jump to conclusions, but clearly Longuet had upset the other members of the community in some way by what the sisters call *indecorous behaviour.* The letter states that he was *repeatedly admonished* but after *refusing to alter his mode of proceeding,* he was asked to *procure himself another lodging.* Longuet himself clearly did not consider he had done anything wrong.

The sisters appear to be suggesting that Longuet is waging some kind of vendetta against the other French priests. It is, however, striking that he continued to officiate at baptisms, marriages and burials at Finch's Buildings throughout the period between his arrival in Reading and the founding of the new chapel. Moreover, he clearly went on enjoying the support of both the Bishops, who themselves seem to have had differences of opinion with the Finch's Buildings community.

No date is given for this incident, but there is a hint as to when it may have occurred in the letter written by Longuet, copied out by the sisters and sent to Poynter, who must have sighed when he read the acrimonious accusations made by both parties. François writes about, *the shameful way with which I was thrown out of my room by him* (Godquin) *at the head of the other French priests; and all of you under his influence.*

He goes on to write, very unkindly we may feel: *Consider the misfortunes which have befallen you since my being turned out of my room and take care not to expose yourselves to anything worse.*

It is highly probable that these 'misfortunes' refer to the suicide of Marianne's husband Thomas Cowslade. He appears to have shot himself, for no obvious reason, in the market place at Andover, in December 1806. A verdict of insanity was returned by the inquest. Cowslade was the co-owner, with Mrs Smart, of the *Reading Mercury.* Unsurprisingly, given the shocking manner of his death, no mention of it appears in the paper and Anna Maria carried on the management of the paper alone until she herself died in May 1809. Even a twentieth century history of the Cowslade family, written by Lucy Harrison, a descendant of the Cowslades, and published in *The Berkshire Archaeological Journal* for 1933, makes no mention of the suicide, which was clearly still regarded as deeply shameful by the family.

It would seem likely, therefore, that Longuet left Finch's Buildings some time before the end of 1806. We do not know where he lived between then and the 23rd of January 1811, the earliest date on which he could have moved into the new house and chapel.

Bishop Poynter's letter from early January 1809 gives us some idea of Longuet's activities in the Reading mission. He clearly loved teaching the children and the Bishop writes that he was *much pleased with the manner in which they answered me in the Catechism.* Poynter's words are probably designed to be read out to the Catechism class as he continues: *I hope they will all continue to attend to your instructions, to be diligent in going to the Chapel, to be devout at their prayers and to give good example by their virtuous behaviour. I pray that almighty God may give his blessing to them all and reward you for all the pains you take with your congregation.*

By the following letter, dated February 20th, it is clear that discussions with Bishop Douglass have taken place and that the 'nitty gritty' subject of finance has been discussed in detail. Clearly Longuet has asked Poynter to advance £200 for the project. Somewhat dryly, perhaps, the Bishop replies: *Not having £200 of my own, I made application for a loan of that sum but was not happy enough to obtain it.*

He suggests that, as Longuet has told him that he expects to be able to raise an extra £200 within three years, it may be *more prudent* to wait till then, *and then see in what manner Providence disposes of things for the great object you have in view.*

As Poynter indicates, money would be required not just to build the chapel but to support the Missionary. Clearly the two Bishops were worried that Longuet might be rushing ahead with his plans too precipitately, but did not wish to discourage him. Poynter ends his letter with prayers that God may bless Longuet's endeavours in Reading. We do not know what transpired immediately but it looks as if Longuet pressed ahead anyway, as eleven months later the Bishop was writing as follows, again urging caution but showing a willingness to proceed if conditions were right:

You inform me that you have found a place, which is freehold, in a convenient part of the town. Before you purchase it, permit me to ask, whether there is any building upon it, which may be converted into a Chapel, or the materials of which may be used for the building of a house & Chapel. It must be considered that a new house & Chapel will cost a large sum of money, that it may be several years before we should be able to raise it; & consequently if the ground you are thinking of purchasing should not be such as will be let for a good rent, you would in the mean time lose the interest of the £300, which you give for the purchase of it. These things are to be considered, also what the building of a house & Chapel would cost. But if no buildings could be found, which might easily be turned into a Chapel, I should think it preferable. You will oblige me by favouring me with your observations on these subjects.

Obviously letters crossed in the post because Poynter writes again on the 25th of January thanking Longuet for his letter (or *favor* as he generally calls a letter), of the 7th of January, in which the priest had clarified certain points of concern. The Bishop now gives permission *that the ground be purchased for £300, according to your proposals to me.* However he stipulates that the deeds must be made out in his (Poynter's) name. Longuet is asked to have the deeds checked by his attorney to examine *whether the title be good* and to tell the Bishop when the contract is ready for signing so that he can either come to Reading or have it sent to him elsewhere.

It is in this letter that we have the first mention of a Sister Lawrence who was presumably helping in the Mission. Poynter also sends his best wishes to *good Mr. Lefèbvre whose kind attention to your concerns I shall remember with gratitude.* This latter was Charles Lefèbvre, the resident priest at Mapledurham, the seat of the Blounts, whose family history he was researching. In letters written after Longuet's death Charles is referred to as *son ami intime* (his close friend), and it seems likely that the two priests often visited each other. Charles, whose second name was Hyacinth, was four years older than his friend and is described in the lists of French priests as a *religieux*. This appears to mean that he was a member of a religious order, but was not a monk. We have one letter from him to Bishop Poynter in which he signs himself simply as C. Lefèbvre, without any extra initials which might indicate to which order he belonged.

Lefèbvre was from the diocese of St. Omer, in what is now the *Nord, Pas de Calais* department, so it is unlikely that he knew Longuet before they left France. His name appears in the Laity's Directory and he is mentioned in Plasse's two volume work *Le clergé français réfugié en Angleterre,* published in 1886, which contains a list, compiled from various sources, of the French priests in England during the Revolution. Poynter obviously regarded him very highly and often asks Longuet to pass on his good wishes.

The Chapel of the Resurrection

As with modern house sales, it would appear that Longuet's first attempt to buy property was not successful, as in August 1810 Poynter writes: *I pray that God may give you patience under all the Disappointments.* He asks that if Longuet finds a house, *convenient for all your purposes,* he should inform the Bishop before considering any bargain. It is in this letter that a new character enters the story.

We can assume that Longuet had been looking for wealthy Catholics who might be willing to give financial support to his new chapel. One possible sponsor, Sir Henry Englefield, patron of the Franciscan priest Father Baynham at Ufton Court, who occasionally celebrated Mass in Reading, had moved away from Whiteknights. This was because of what Miss Cowslade calls *the offensive prejudices of the neighbouring Gentry.* Father Baynham had remained at the empty mansion of Ufton Court when the Perkins, the Catholic family who owned it, left the district. According to Longuet, in a later letter (6th of June 1812), Father Baynham had offered to pass on the allowance to Longuet who had refused it *knowing he* (Baynham) had *hardly enough to live upon.* It appears that after Baynham's death the allowance had been paid to the Smarts and Cowslades, much to Longuet's disgust. Although Poynter did eventually intervene to secure the money for Longuet, it is clear that Sir Henry was, as it were, in the Smart/Cowslade camp. It was necessary to look elsewhere.

The new sponsor for Longuet's project was Francis Gallini, of Yattendon, near Newbury. His father was the great dancer, choreographer and impresario Giovanni Andrea Battista Gallini, the owner of the King's Theatre in the Haymarket, who, with Johann Peter Salomon, had persuaded Joseph Haydn to come to London. Giovanni, who had been awarded the title Knight of the Golden Spur by the Pope after a successful performance, and was George III's ballet teacher, had married into the English aristocracy through his marriage to the daughter of the Third Earl of Abingdon in 1763.

Francis was the younger of her twin sons, born in 1766. When Giovanni died in 1805 his estate was valued at £150,000, a vast sum which was divided between John and Francis, his sons, and his daughters Joyce Ann and Louise. In consequence, Francis was an extremely wealthy man of 44 when he is first mentioned in Poynter's letter of the 13th of August 1810. The Bishop sends his compliments to Gallini and tells him that his son is *very well*. This would indicate that the boy was a student at St Edmund's, which was a boarding school as well as a seminary. On a later occasion Poynter promises to bring *Master Gallini* with him when he visits Reading to sign the legal papers for the property purchase. It is very possible that Longuet had been tutoring the boy at home before he went to Old Hall Green.

By January of 1811 Poynter was able to write: *The house which is offered to you seems very convenient, & I hope that you will make it answer. You may, if you please, have the purchase made in my name. But only describe me as the Rev. or Doctor Poynter, of Old Hall Green, in the Parish of Standon, Herts.*

It is puzzling that the letter only refers to a house, not to a chapel or even to a plot on which a chapel could be built. However we do have one clue as to the relative positions of the house and chapel. Next to this letter, in the archive file in Kensington, is an envelope, addressed to *Rev'd Mr Longuet, Reading, Berks.* It is postmarked *Ware* but the date is unfortunately illegible. On it is drawn an extremely rough sketch of a three story house with an adjoining building. This has a steeply pitched roof and a single round-arched door to its right. The fact that it has been preserved may indicate that this is the only surviving picture of the house and chapel.

Envelope sketch: possibly of house and chapel.

It is possible, perhaps likely, that the chapel was built next to the house after the purchase was made. In a letter to the Abbé Foucher in 1820 Poynter refers to Longuet's having *raised the means of establishing a new Chapel for the Congregation & an adjoining house for the Clergyman.*

Note that Poynter insists that the purchase should be made in his name, not that of Longuet. Subsequent events were to prove the wisdom of this decision. It is also worth noting that Poynter does not wish his episcopal title to be used in a legal document.

Events must have moved quickly as only a month later, on February 4th 1811, Poynter wrote thanking Longuet for *giving me an account of the completion of the purchase of the Premises for a house and Chapel.* It is clear that Mr Gallini was a trustee, as the letter goes on: *I suppose you will have a declaration of Trust to be signed by Mr Gallini, by which he declares that he holds this not as his own property, but in trust for me and the Revd Dr Douglass.*

Poynter asks Longuet to thank Gallini for *his great kindness and zeal in promoting the good of your Congregation.* He tells the priest to ensure that the chapel is *perfectly dry* before it is occupied. Presumably this is a reference to wet plaster. No doubt there was still a good deal of work to be done before the chapel could be used, as the Bishop states he will not come to Reading until at least two weeks after Easter, once Longuet has let him know how things stand.

This letter contains the first hint that all is not well in the relationship between Longuet and the other French priests in Finch's Buildings. Poynter writes: *With respect to the venerable French priests at Reading I trust that you all endeavour to accommodate each other and to make one another as comfortable as possible.* Probably this refers to the dispute about the chapel furnishings, which must have been coming to a head about this time with the imminent transfer of services to the new chapel.

He adds, in Latin: *Carry each other's burdens and so make Christ's kingdom greater,* before sending his sincere regard to *those respectable clergymen whom I saw,* and to Sister Lawrence. It is not clear whether the clergymen to whom he refers are the French priests. They may even have been Protestant ministers, with whom Longuet was on friendly terms.

Presumably unknown to Longuet, Thomas Webster, the English priest at Woolhampton, had written to Poynter on the 21st of January on the subject of the dispute between Longuet and the Finch's Buildings community, particularly Godquin. It is clear that the bad feeling was deep rooted. He quotes an incident when the two priests were in the same room, that of a sick parishioner, *and in presence of some Protestants*, and Longuet refused even to *move his hat* after being *respectfully saluted* by Godquin. It is very clear that Webster's sympathies are with the older priest and his colleagues, whom he describes as *quiet, peaceable and in no way disposed to encroach on any privilege or right he may have or persuade himself he has.*

Note the somewhat barbed tone. Clearly Webster and Longuet were not on good terms with each other. Webster refers to a reported comment of Longuet's that Webster should mind his congregation and Longuet would mind his own.

Webster gives examples of Longuet's shocking behaviour. One particularly striking incident is when François allows women and girls to serve at Mass:

His requiring women and girls present to repeat together aloud the answers in the serving at Mass is thought absurd. One of the latter, whom he taught to serve, answering so loud as to be troublesome to others in the Chapel, was approached by a respectable person and desired in a low tone of voice to answer in a different manner. He observing this saying (sic) *in an audible & seemingly irritable manner "Nancy go on".*

Given that allowing girls on the altar was considered revolutionary even in the late twentieth century, this is an extraordinary testament to Longuet's very open-minded approach to his ministry. It seems very likely that the incident which led to his being asked to leave his apartment in Finch's Buildings may have been of this nature.

It also appears that Longuet had been celebrating Midnight Mass at Christmas, a practice which was obviously considered unwise. According to Webster there had been *confusion & improper conduct* at this service in 1807 which he, Webster, must have reported to Bishop Douglass. The Vicar Apostolic had instructed Longuet, via Webster, that he should stop celebrating Christmas Mass at midnight. This injunction had been obeyed for two years but *notwithstanding such prohibition, he took upon him this last Christmas to say it at Midnight again.*

It is extraordinary to think that these incidents must have happened in the Finch's Buildings chapel while Longuet was living elsewhere and refusing to communicate with his former community. The French priests were probably using Webster to pass their grievances on to Bishop Poynter and, ultimately, to Bishop Douglass, who was clearly unwell and had asked Webster to write to Poynter instead. Webster complains about *the untrue use he, Mr Longuet, had made of your expressions when at Reading.* So it would appear that Poynter had, while visiting Reading, said something which Longuet had interpreted as support for his position. Without independent reports, it is impossible to say to what extent Webster's and Godquin's complaints were justified. It is, however, striking that Poynter's letters to Longuet are very positive; full of support and encouragement for the young priest, even while urging him to be prudent. It certainly appears, however, that François could be harsh and uncharitable to those who had offended him. Webster gives an example of this, his exclamation marks an indication of how shocking he found it: *On another occasion on a Sunday after the Confiteor had been said at Mass for one, whom the preceeding* (sic) *day he had given absolution but with whom he was displeased, turning his head and seeing the intended communicant, he refuses* (sic) *to give the Holy Communion!!*

Webster is particularly appalled that Longuet should show *insolence and contempt* to his elders: *It may not be improper to add further that all are older and Mr Godquin now more than 60 years old has spent 23 of them with respect as Vicar or curate abroad and in his manners most humble, pacific & mild.* Godquin was, in fact, 65 at the time.

Further hints of discord appear in Poynter's next letter, dated the 3rd of March. It is an answer to two letters from Longuet, both of which had been shown by Poynter to the Vicar Apostolic, John Douglass. While both Bishops profess themselves *much pleased* with Longuet's work in building the Reading mission, they urge him to *carry on the good work in such a prudent manner to unite all the faithful in the bonds of peace.*

Obviously there were also anxieties as to how the opening of the new chapel would be received by the non-Catholic majority of Reading's population. Longuet, writes Poynter, must be careful, *not to give any offence to the Protestants by making too much éclat. In raising a new Chapel where there had been none for a long time, great prudence is necessary.*

Poynter instructs Longuet to see to the legal procedures of licensing both chapel and *officiating Clergyman* at the Quarter Sessions in Reading *in a manner agreeable to the Act of Parliament in favour of Catholics in the year 1791.*

No doubt the wish for not too much *éclat* is one reason why there appears to be no report in the *Mercury* about the opening of the new chapel. The other is most likely to be the worsening state of relations between Longuet and the Smart daughters, Marianne Cowslade and Elizabeth Lenoir, whose mother had died in 1809, leaving the ownership of the *Reading Mercury* in their hands.

We know that the new chapel was named *The Chapel of the Resurrection* or *Resurrection Chapel*. The name presumably makes reference to the return of Catholicism to Reading after the destruction of the Abbey. The Cowslade Manuscript refers to *a little edifice* (*to which the Founder had given the name of the 'Resurrection Chapel'*) but an 1813 entry in the Reading Registers refers to the marriage between James Earles and Maria Cooper on June the 18^{th,} 1813 as *the first in the chapel of the Resurrection.* It is thus unclear which of the two forms, *Resurrection Chapel* or *Chapel of the Resurrection,* was normally used. It is a nice linguistic joke that the pub which is believed to be on the site of the chapel should be called 'The Rising Sun'.

The name, *Resurrection Chapel,* first appears in the *Laity's Directory* for 1812 with the following entry:

Reading, Berks., Vastern Lane. Resurrection Chapel, under the patronage of the R.R. W. Poynter and F. Gallini Esq. of Yattendon. Mass at 11 o'clock; Discourse after it. Vespers at 3 on Sundays and Feasts of Obligation. Chaplain Rev. Mr. Longuet.

This entry obviously worried Bishop Poynter. He was known for his conciliatory nature; (his successor, James Bramston, compared him to a bee *with a sting to use only when necessity requires, but constantly productive of much honey*), but he clearly felt that Longuet had acted rashly in describing Gallini as a patron of the new chapel. He had already, in March the previous year, written as follows:

With respect to your offering to Mr Gallini or to any person whatever the compliment of presenting a Priest for the Chapel, Bp. Douglass begs that you will not think of such a thing: he totally disapproves of it. We shall be happy to acknowledge the pious zeal which the good Mr Gallini shews in promoting the work & we pray that he and you may have a great reward in heaven. Your sentiments of submission are very pleasing.

It would be fascinating to know to what Longuet was 'submitting'. In a letter dated the 31st of January 1812, in the nearest he comes to a rebuke, Poynter wrote:

I must beg leave to observe that if you directed Mrs Hastings (presumably in charge of compiling the entries for the directory) to announce the Chapel of Reading to be under the Patronage of any Lay Gentleman, you were not in order. You do not find that any Chapels are announced as being under the Patronage of Dr Douglass & of any Lay Gentleman. Mr Gallini is the last Gentleman who would wish to depart from what is usually observed. Next year the advertisement may be put in order.

The Dispute between Longuet and the Smart Sisters

It is very noticeable how careful Poynter and Douglass are to avoid transgressing the law or offending public opinion in any way. They must therefore have been horrified at the bombshell which broke over them in April 1811 when a letter arrived, signed by both Marianne and Elizabeth, and including a copy of a letter from Longuet to them. The letter to Poynter is written by Elizabeth, who refers to her sister's having been handed the *indecent* letter as she was coming out of his Mass, presumably still at the old chapel in Finch's Buildings. It would appear that Longuet had asked for the chapel furnishings at Finch's buildings to be moved into the new chapel. The Smarts sent back a note (quoted verbatim by Elizabeth) to say that certain items were their private property and should be left in the old chapel, though they were happy for him to take a *fine crucifix* presented to them by *the governor of Monte Video* (sic).

Elizabeth's letter fills two closely written pages and reminds Poynter of how Mrs Smart and her daughters had been responsible for bringing the Finch's Buildings priests to Reading, furnishing the house and chapel and making up the cost of the rent and taxes, which she quotes as being about £20 a year, beyond the money supplied by Sir Henry Englefield, *till the period of a heavy misfortune which befell my sister about four years ago.*

The letter implies that as a result of this misfortune, presumably Thomas Cowslade's suicide, Mrs Smart had been unable to continue the same level of support for the French priests. Her death may well have been hastened by grief at the family tragedy.

Elizabeth begins her letter: *Every person who has seen the letter of which I herewith enclose you a copy is of opinion that it ought to be laid before you.*

Longuet, meanwhile, had also been sharing correspondence with his friends and parishioners. In his own letter, carefully copied out by Elizabeth, he writes: *Those who have already seen what you and Mr Godequin* (sic) *sent me say "Now we see plainly how ill you have been treated".*

Clearly the dispute had divided the Catholic community into two camps: those, including the Finch's Buildings priests under Godquin, who sided with the Smart family, and Longuet's supporters. It is evident from the tone of both letters that feelings were running very high. Longuet harks back to *the shameful way with which I was thrown out of my room by him* (Godquin) *at the head of the other French priests; and all of you under his influence.*

He continues: *I have still the letters of your Mother. I keep everything by me with design to publish everything which has been done for & against the foundation from the moment I began to be appointed at the head of the Congregation.*

It is not surprising that in a later letter Poynter suggests that *it will be best to have all the writings kept here, together with all the other writings of the District.* Nor, perhaps, should we be amazed that none of these letters from Mrs Smart, which Longuet was intending to publish, has been kept for posterity. Probably they were destroyed or held in a secret archive of some kind by the Bishop. It is hard not to feel a certain sympathy for both parties. Clearly Longuet felt aggrieved at the way he had been treated years before, but he also seems to have believed he was justified in asking for the altar furnishings and other equipment from Finch's Buildings, since *they have been used by every french* (sic) *priest these eight years without exception in that room which has served for all the Congregation, and for no other reason because it is to be removed in a more convenient place and more adapted for the purpose.*

Unfortunately the wax seals on this part of the letter have obscured parts of Longuet's writing but he appeals to the sisters to consider how they will be viewed by posterity and, more seriously, how they will fare at the Last Judgement since they would not even supply *a dirty rag* (presumably altar linen), for the benefit of the chapel and its congregation.

In his impassioned appeal to the sisters Longuet becomes first eloquent, then somewhat incoherent: *Consider that I meet with no Protestant but wishes me good success & many give a very generous assistance, no Catholic but those who you influenced by your example, behave so to me. All give me encouragement as much as they can, should you be the only ones to disgrace yourselves!*

Unfortunately Longuet goes on to suggest that the misfortunes suffered by the Smart family have somehow been caused by the way they have treated him. He asserts that he has both Bishops on his side: *You can easily see how fortunate I have been since, happy because I am in good terms not only with Bishop Douglass, but also with the good Coadjutor who favours me particularly with his protection, and to whom I have given all my little fortune for the benefit of the Catholics of Reading & of course for yourselves: extremely happy!*

The tone becomes ever more impassioned and biblical: *Now in the most supreme degree, because I owe all to God only & nothing to men therefore I say, if Almighty God continues to bless me as he has done these eight years, and if he vouchsafe to protect my favourite foundation I care for nobody who tries or wishes to oppose it. I beg of him to make me resemble his Son who was surrounded only by Poor People, with these I delight to be.*

The letter concludes with a prophecy followed, rather bathetically, by an invitation to call and view the Bishops' letters: *But I have let you know, Mrs Cowslade, that if you do not change your mind before the Bishop comes who very likely will disappoint you & your priests, I shall return you your 5£* (sic) *fearing that it should bring upon my foundation the curse of God instead of his mercy. You have made me a Prophet because I have foretold that, from a long while --- If you wish to be convinced of what I say, favour me with a call and I will show you the letters of the Bishop and the Coadjutor.*

The £5 to which Longuet refers was, Elizabeth explains in her letter, *for seats in his Chapel for which we were likewise to pay a rent.*

In a postscript Longuet, who appears to have calmed down somewhat, writes: *Mrs Cowslade & Mrs Le Noir, in the name of God, for his glory, for your honour and credit and the eternal welfare of your souls I humbly beg of you to reflect and see everything in a more proper light; for this purpose I send you all my blessing and may the Almighty God have mercy on you and assist you with his grace. I remain with the true affection of a Pastor who sincerely wishes the salvation of your souls.*

It is not surprising that Marianne and Elizabeth reacted badly to Longuet's letter. To make matters worse, as Elizabeth wrote: *the indecent Letter I complain of was delivered to my Sister yesterday as she was coming out from his Mass; and was consequently planned by him before it. What a disposition for the Sacrifice!*

The sisters obviously believed that Longuet was intending to persuade the Bishops that the old chapel should be closed when the new one opened. Elizabeth had clearly been sharing her anxieties with Webster as she writes: *Mr Webster has given us hopes that you will allow the old Chapel to remain, tho' I know Mr Longuet will do his utmost to prevail upon you to abolish it. I trust there is no risk of his succeeding.*

In the event the old chapel clearly did remain after the new one opened. We do not know when it eventually closed. Godquin died in 1818, only a year after Longuet, while Gondré lived on until 1827. The remaining two priests, Le Tellier and La Noë, had their licenses to say Mass revoked in 1818 as a result of their Blanchardist views.

Poynter seems to have acted swiftly to defuse the situation. On the 24th of May he wrote to Longuet that he had spoken to Sir Henry Englefield who had left the chapel furniture at his (Poynter's) disposal. He asks Longuet to send him a full list of all the articles and promises to send directions as to their disposal as soon as possible. He must have written to Webster around the same time as a letter from the latter thanks the bishop for *the explicit and satisfactory instructions you have condescended to favour me with by which I am entitled to act with more clearness and confidence in the affairs at Reading.*

Webster continues: *I have been there twice within these four days with the intention of relieving the minds of Mesdames Cowslade & Le Noir also of seeing Mr Longuet who on both occasions happened to be from home. I will take the first opportunity in my power to see him, which in consequence of his peculiar disposition I prefer to writing. In the meantime I have put in a caveat to the removal of any Chapel things not his own.*

CHAPTER 3

The Opening of the Chapel 1811 – 1812

The Chapel, the House and its Furnishings

In his letter of the 24th of May Bishop Poynter had regretted that he would be unable to visit Reading to see the new chapel until June 29th, the feast of Saints Peter and Paul, because of his commitments both at Ware and in London, where Bishop Douglass' health was continuing to decline.

Poynter's letter dated June 11th begins with formal instructions: *The furniture of the Chapel which is acknowledged to have been brought by Sir Henry Inglefield* (sic*) may be removed to the New Chapel as soon as you think proper. If anything is contested I wish it to be removed even from the Old Chapel, without the decision of Mr Webster. The benches which belong to Sir H. Inglefield* (sic) *must not be altered.*

Note the words *without the decision of Mr Webster*. We may suspect that Poynter is somewhat exasperated with both parties but is irritated by Webster's interventions. We can only guess what 'alterations' Longuet may have been proposing for the benches.

Poynter's visit is clearly imminent. He promises to bring Master Gallini with him, after sending his *best and kindest compliments* to the boy's father, and accepts Longuet's invitation to stay at the house.

At this point it is appropriate to discuss what we know about the house itself. A document from October 1817, in the aftermath of Longuet's death, contains a detailed description of the building and its contents. From it we know that there were three downstairs parlours, described as right, left and back, plus a kitchen. Upstairs there was a *Back Bowed Bedroom* plus two further 'bedchambers', front and back, and an attic.

The list of contents gives a good indication that Longuet lived comfortably, if not in luxury. The right hand parlour contained six japanned chairs, a *Scotch carpet,* a mahogany flap table and a *Cherry tree dining table* plus a *Pantheon stove* equipped with shovel, tongs and a poker. There was a similar stove in the back parlour. This is where most of the serving dishes seem to have been kept. They included *5 china and 10 Wedgewood plates* and *a tureen and ladle.* Wedgewood's factory had been set up in 1759 and by 1812 was producing bone china, which may have been what Longuet owned. Other tableware included 3 decanters, 4 ale glasses, 2 teapots, cups and saucers, a cruet set and a jug. There were also two canisters, possibly for tea and coffee or chocolate, and a toasting fork. The left parlour, which was, perhaps Longuet's study, contained a reading desk and another *Scotch carpet*, what is described as a *Bath grate* and a steel fender, with tongs and a poker. It is unlikely that Longuet did his own cooking so presumably a servant worked in the kitchen, which was equipped with *2 boiling pots, saucepan, coffee pot, frying pan, baking dish* as well as a washtub and ironing equipment. There was also a kitchen grate and a meat safe. As always, it is the precise domestic details which are so fascinating.

Upstairs there were three bedrooms, one of which is described as the *Back Bowed Bedroom*, probably used for visitors such as Bishop Poynter. It contained a *stump bedstead* with a mattress, four *walnut tree* chairs and a matching settle or settee, a bookshelf and a deal table. The bed was equipped with 2 pillows, 2 blankets, a cotton quilt and what is described as a *Marseilles counterpane*.

The front bedchamber was presumably Longuet's own as it contained many personal items such as two brushes, a razor and a comb, which he must have left behind when he set out for Wallingford on February 13th, 1812, expecting to return the same evening. We know that the curtains were of *blue stuff* and that his feather bed was covered with a check-patterned quilt. Other equipment included a *rule and powder*, possibly for care of a wig, and a bootjack. The room also contained a wainscot bureau and a basin, stand and jug for washing. For reading there was a japanned candlestick. We even know that he possessed three towels. The bath itself was in the back bedchamber, together with *two draining boards*.

There was also an attic bedroom, presumably for one or more servants, simply equipped with two stump bedsteads and a straw paliasse.

Unfortunately this document has been affected by water damage and it is not possible to make out all the details, but it does give us a vivid and, in retrospect, poignant picture of how Longuet lived.

We have a lawyer's bill, which gives us precise dates for the purchase of the new premises. The entry for January 6th 1811 reads:

	£	s	d
Attending you upon your agreement with the			
Miss Tyrrells to purchase the House & Premises			
in Vastern Lane & upon them for the title deeds			
when they declared same.		*6*	*8*
Perusing and examining the several deeds relating			
to the title of the said Premises	*1*	*1*	*0*
Attending you and taking Instructions for an			
Assignment thereof		*6*	*8*

Drawing draft & Assignment to the Reverend
Dr Poynter & Francis Gallini Esq. Trustees
for you.   Col 34   1   14   0
Fair copy & engraving thereof   1   14   0
Stamps & Parchment   3   18   0

Note that Francis Gallini and Doctor Poynter are named as trustees.

The sale was completed on the 23rd of January, as the bill reads:

23rd Attending reading over & attending the Execution
         of Assignment by the Misses Tyrrell & completing
         Final Settlement of this business   13   4

The lawyer, Mr John Richards, also charged for his advice relating to the licensing of
the building for worship:

You having created a Building intended for religious worship attending you & Mr
Gallini upon the subject of Certifying same to the Quarter Sessions as required by
Act of 31Geo 3rd c32

Perusing & considering said Act in order to
Prepare the accepting Certificate   6   8
Drawing Certificate   5   0
Attending you & Mr Gallini thereon   6   8
Fair copy Certificate & engraving done on Parchment   5   0

Entries for April and May relate to attending the Quarter Sessions at which Longuet
took *the oaths appointed by the Acts* and the certificate was recorded. The court fees
came to 15 shillings.

The final entry reads:

June 15th Attending Dr Poynter, Mr Gallini & yourself
           This day upon the subject of this business   6   8

In all, the bill came to £12. 19s 0d, of which nine pounds were paid by cash, *at
sundry times,* leaving a balance of £3. 19. 0d which was finally paid in February
1814.

A roughly torn scrap of paper preserved with the other letters contains a request to
Poynter and Gallini to repay £219 to a Mr Joseph Boralo in the event of Longuet's
death. Presumably this relates to a loan from another parishioner of Italian descent.

We have been unable to trace who this gentleman was. On the reverse of the document Longuet agrees to pay: *Lawful Interest for the Same till the Whole of the Principal be Discharged.* An almost illegible note in the bottom right hand corner appears to begin: *In the Case of Death direct my Trustees .....*

Life at the Chapel of the Resurrection

Practical problems connected with the setting up of the new chapel dominate some of the letters from early 1812. Unfortunately at this point we still only have Poynter's letters to Longuet which were later returned to London. François was clearly concerned that the vestments from the old chapel, which had originated from Englefield House, were no longer fit to be used. The Bishop offered to send him money to buy new ones, from a five-guinea donation he had been given *for the purchase of vestments.* The old vestments, adds Poynter, must not be burnt but put aside until his next visit to Reading. It would appear that Longuet did not immediately comply with these instructions as in the next letter Poynter writes, with pointed underlining: *I think I told you that the five pounds I sent you were for the purchase of vestments for your Chapel, if so employ it in vestments, that the intentions of Donors may be complied with.*

The new chapel's paten (the plate used to hold the sacred host) needed mending and would have to be sent back to London to be re-blessed by the Bishop before it could be used again. Much of the letter is taken up with the forms of Baptism, conditional or absolute, to be used for two young boys who may possibly already have been baptised as Anglicans. As before the Bishop appears anxious not to offend non-Catholics by *too much éclat.* He asks that the boys should be baptised privately, with only one godfather.

The question of whether Mr. Gallini was to be considered a patron of the chapel clearly continued to worry the Bishop. In his letter dated the 31st of January 1812 Poynter again wrote warmly about him: *I shall always feel grateful to Mr. Gallini for all he has done in favour of the Chapel & shall remember with pleasure his edifying example in supporting the true worship of God in Reading.*

However he went on to write: *I trust you perfectly understand that it will be under my Patronage & superintendancy & that of the Vicar Apostolic for the London District.*

Longuet was clearly not in submissive mood on this question as in March the Bishop refers to the priest's *observations concerning the chapels which are under Bp. Douglass' Patronage,* and points out that several chapels whose accounts were laid before Bishop Douglass were not announced in the Directory as being under Douglass' patronage. Perhaps Longuet felt that to be under Poynter's name, rather than that of the Vicar Apostolic himself, was to be seen as less important. The Bishop was at pains to point out that Douglass, who was at the time seriously ill, (he died less than two months later), *considers me as, una Persona, with himself & therefore has freely left the direction & superintendence of your chapel to me.*

The next few words hint at the continuing 'bad blood' between Longuet and the Finch's Buildings priests: *But if there are any people in Reading, who imagine that there is any division of sentiments or views between Bp. Douglass & me, I must request them to be convinced of the contrary & that I should positively condemn those words vous avez Poynter mais ils ont Douglass.* (Underlined in the original French and meaning, "You have Poynter but they have Douglass"). *We both share one & the same object, the glory of our God to be promoted through the establishment of his worship & the salvation of souls, we seek this by underlined means & efforts.*

We cannot be sure to whom *any people in Reading* refers, but it is likely to be Marianne and Elizabeth or possibly Webster who, as we have seen, was suspicious of Longuet.

In 1812 Bishop William Poynter succeeded John Douglass as Vicar Apostolic of the London District and the remaining documents, which now include letters from Longuet himself, are kept in a separate file in the Westminster archives. Though nine years Longuet's senior, Poynter seems to have possessed similar qualities of initiative and drive and was probably able to understand François' impetuous nature. His years in France meant he was thoroughly at home in the French language and he was also proficient in Italian as well as Latin. Longuet's English, after twenty years in England, is very fluent but the occasional grammatical quirk reminds us that he is not a native speaker. In one letter he appears to use French for a confidential matter. No doubt he retained a French accent all his life.

In a letter written by Poynter soon after his appointment as Vicar Apostolic he begins by praising Longuet for the work he is doing in Reading: *I congratulate with you and return thanks to Almighty God for the success which you have experienced in the establishment of your Chapel. The effects of your charitable exertions will long be felt by the Catholics at Reading. They will be gratefully remembered by me and, I trust, will be eternally rewarded by the great Pastor of Souls, our Saviour and our God.*

Clearly Poynter had recently visited Reading as he reminds Longuet that during his last visit the priest had shown him Bishop Douglass' ordinance *relative to private chapels in which French priests have leave to say Mass.* He asks Longuet to send him a copy, as he cannot lay his hands on the document.

The first of Longuet's surviving letters to Poynter is dated the 6th of June 1812 and begins *Mon très cher Evèque,* (My very dear Bishop), an indication of the warm relationship between the two men. It begins with an urgent plea for guidance in dealing with a prisoner in the gaol. This is written in French, possibly because of its confidential nature. In translation the letter begins, *I beg you to answer this question urgently: is a man accused and found guilty of passing false coinage and asked by his judge to give the name of the forger (coiner) obliged in conscience to name him whatever the consequences, given that many people would be put at risk of hanging and consequently perhaps more than a hundred people would have their reputation destroyed. Note that the criminal would obviously be unable to prove his denunciation and moreover that would not remedy the crime.*

Poynter's reply, written in early July 1812, indicates he may have felt somewhat alarmed that Longuet was at risk of falling foul of the British legal system. He warns Longuet: *You must be careful not to direct those under your care to do more than the forms of our Courts and the spirit of our Constitution requires,* and promises that Mr Webster will come and explain all this to him, *which will be done more satisfactorily by word of mouth than can properly be done by letter.*

Given what we know about the mutual suspicion of the two priests, this may not have been an easy meeting. Longuet's letter goes on to describe how he has converted one of the prisoners who has *boldly confessed the Catholic faith* before going to his place of transportation, presumably Australia.

François' attitude to the prisoners is remarkable: *I make myself like one of them, being perhaps great deal more criminal than them before Almighty God and I have been favoured by Heaven as to have gained their affection, with the assistance of respectable Protestants my generous friends who deserve to be looked upon as true Samaritans.*

We already know, from Longuet's letter to Marianne and Elizabeth, that he was on better terms with some Protestants than with certain sections of the Catholic community and it is now notable that Longuet appears to be working with Protestant clergy in his ministry to the prisoners. It is difficult to know how normal this ecumenical cooperation was at the time but tributes to him after his death suggest that it was considered exceptional.

This same letter suggests that the dispute with the Smart family was still alive over a year after the acrimonious exchanges of April 1811. Longuet felt that an allowance paid by Sir Henry Englefield to Father Baynham, the resident priest at Ufton Court, should have been transferred to him after Father Baynham's death but that the Smart family were holding on to the money. It is worth quoting this part of the letter in full as it gives us an interesting insight into Longuet's career as a tutor. Unfortunately some words are missing as the page is torn.

I happened last week to meet by chance with Mr Blandy who does business for Sir Henry Englefield for the purpose of putting his (Blandy's) *son under my tuition for French and Latin, having heard of him before I ...* (missing words)... *liberty to ask him what he did with the Mission money which Sir Henry allowed for the Priest of the Congregation. There ten years* (probably a translation of the French 'il y a dix ans', meaning ten years ago) *I was appointed by the late Revd. Mr Baynham who willingly wanted to give it to me but I refused it knowing he had hardly enough to live upon, but he being dead these nine years, he was no more in want of it; he showed me his book and I saw the names of the late Mrs Smart and then the name of Mrs. Lenoir who received the last five pounds in January this year.*

I after that showed him the four lines of your last letter but one; that you had done your part to favour me in getting these ten pounds, that before the French priests and publicly in the chapel in your sermon you had nominated me the Pastor of the congregation and promised me in the hearing of Mr Monk and a Nun who was in my house I was to have that money; therefore I begged him not to pay the five pounds which are now due but to write to Sir Henry about it.

*If it is the good pleasure of Sir Henry to make his promise good I must have it, but on the contrary if he prefers to favour those women with it let it be but I trust to Providence who has always been very merciful upon me and has given me very generous friends among Protestants, may God Almighty bring them to the light of his true faith that their good works may not (*illegible*) them but may profit them for everlasting life.*

In the reply to this letter, dated the 7th of July, Bishop Poynter promises to speak to Sir Henry about the allowance the next time he sees him. Not surprisingly these disputes do not feature in the account written by Miss Cowslade, Marianne's daughter, in the 1840s, and there is no hint of any animosity, so it is to be assumed relations subsequently improved.

It is clear that the relationship between Longuet and Poynter developed into a real friendship. By January 1813 Longuet is thanking the Bishop for a New Year's gift (not a Christmas present as might be expected today). He writes: *I never read anything that has given me greater pleasure, I tell you sincerely that I take it as a true master peace* (sic) *of Christian eloquence, I have spoken in the same way to many people with great success, for I have had 14 new converts these six months 2 married men, 3 married women; 5 boys, 4 girls.*

From this we can deduce that the present was a book of sermons. We have a complete list of the books in Longuet's library (see Appendix C) and it contains several volumes of sermons, including a seven-volume collection of the sermons of James Archer (1751-1832), comprising homilies for all the Sundays and major festivals of the liturgical year. Other titles include the ten volumes of Butler's *Lives of the Saints,* Gobinet's *Instructions de la jeunesse* and a five volume edition of the Douai Bible, plus many volumes on Theology, a Latin *Catechism of Christian Doctrine* and *Webbes* (sic) *Plainchant.*

From a letter written by Longuet's friend Charles Lefèbvre, after his death, we know that Longuet intended this *Mission Library* to be kept in the parish but sadly it seems to have been claimed by his family in France.

Longuet reports that he has reduced his debts to £80. The remission of the debt, presumably on the chapel, is a recurrent theme in the letters and was obviously of great concern both to Longuet and to the Vicar Apostolic, who often refers to it in his letters.

The rest of the letter shows Longuet taking the initiative, perhaps a little too strongly, in his dealings with his flock:

I beg the favour of your Lordship to allow me to say Mass at Yattenton (sic. presumably Yattendon) *in Mr Gallini's House, he being unwell for I go once a week in his Neighbourhood, I shall take care that everything shall be properly and decently done and as they are at a great distance from a Chapel to change the obligation of the Sunday into that Mass provided they keep the Sunday as they ought and to give them communion, this I should prefer to* ...(This word, probably a place name, is illegible and was probably so to Poynter as well, as it has been underlined), *if it is possible, he keeps Catholic servants.*

Poynter must have been somewhat alarmed at the idea of Longuet changing the day of obligation from Sunday into Wednesday. His answering letter has not been preserved but a note in the corner of Longuet's letter, written in Poynter's handwriting, reads: *Sunday's obligation must remain - you may say Mass at Mr Gallini's house providing all be decent.*

It is unclear whether Mr Gallini, despite his poor health, was expected to travel to Reading to attend Sunday Mass. A further annotation by Poynter, presumably a query to his secretary, asks where exactly 'Yattenton' is and whether it is in the London Distrct. He may have wondered whether it came under the jurisdiction of John Milner, Vicar Apostolic for the Midland District, with whom he was in dispute over how Catholic Emancipation could best be achieved.

A postscript gives the information that 174 people had been 'reckoned' in the chapel the previous month. More details of numbers are given in the last surviving letter from Longuet to Poynter, dated the 9th of May, 1813: *I send you by this account of what has passed in our chapel since last Easter; eleven children have been baptised, two men, three women, five children baptised under condition; two men and two women read their abjuration, one is dead, thirty seven received the Paschal communion in our chapel this year.*

It should be remembered that at this period, before the reforms of Pius X in the early 20th century, frequent communion was not the norm and children did not receive the Eucharist, so numbers of communicants cannot be taken as indicating the size of the congregation. What we do not know is how many people were still attending Mass at the 'Old Chapel'.

The men and women who 'read their abjuration' were presumably abjuring their Anglican faith. Later in the letter Longuet talks of having about a dozen adults preparing for confirmation and he assures Poynter that *they went neither near the Bishop nor with any intention of receiving anything.* Presumably this must refer to the Anglican bishop. Longuet goes on to describe the pattern of services: *We continue the same exercises as last year viz. Mass at eleven, vespers at three and evening prayers at seven in the evening, a lecture in the morning and an exhortation extemporary in the evening, the chapel is pretty well attended at all times and very full in the morning...*

This is the same list of services as the one given in the Laity's Directory. He assures Poynter that he is continuing to reduce the debt on the chapel and hopes to have it down to £50 by August. Longuet also reports that he keeps the house *in as good repair as I can.*

It is clear that many letters are missing, as the next one in the archives, from Poynter to Longuet, dated the 20th of January 1814, is the last before Longuet's death three years later. Poynter congratulates him on being *so near the term of your alleviation from the burden of your debt,* and goes on to say that *the mission in general and the congregation at Reading in particular will be under great obligation to you for your charitable exertions in raising that Chapel.*

Poynter asks Longuet to pass on his very sincere regard to Mrs Aston. The identity of this lady is unclear but in a letter written by Poynter after Longuet's death she is described as *la bonne religieuse Mme Aston* – the good nun, Mrs Aston. Just as priests were usually referred to as *Mr* so nuns of the time were normally called *Mrs* or *Madam*. She obviously worked with Longuet in the parish but it is not clear exactly in what capacity. Poynter ends his letter: *With every kind sentiment to you and Mrs Aston, I am etc.* Unfortunately the series of letters ends here. Presumably the correspondence continued for the following three years until the shocking and tragic events of February 1817.

CHAPTER 4

Longuet's Death and its Aftermath

Longuet's Murder

On February the 17th, 1817 the *Reading Mercury* which was, as earlier stated, owned and printed by the Catholic Smart-Cowslade family, carried the following sensational announcement, followed by an official appeal:

Thursday evening last Rev. Mr Longuet, a most worthy and much respected gentleman of this town, on his return from Wallingford, where he had been attending his professional duties as a Teacher of the French language, was cruelly murdered about three miles on the Pangbourne Road. – An inquest was taken on the body this day and adjourned till Monday. Some information transpired, which we forbear to mention as it may in the present state of the business defeat the ends of justice. For particulars of this dreadful affair, see advertisement.

MURDER AND ROBBERY
Two Hundred Guineas Reward

Whereas on Thursday evening the Rev. Mr Longuet on his return on horseback from Wallingford was barbarously murdered and robbed between the hours of 7 and 8 o'clock on the Oxford Road about 3 miles from Reading, his head was nearly severed from his body and several dreadful gashes were inflicted on the skull, supposed with a sword, and 5 stabs on the body one of which penetrated the heart. The Murder is conjectured to have been perpetrated by a person well-skilled in the use of the broadsword.

The Assassins plundered the body of 13 guineas as follows. A £10 note of the Wallingford bank: £1 notes of the Bank of England, out of the 4 following numbers 21,793 - 76,613 - 73,674 - 41,103 – Ten shillings of the new coin and a 3s bank token.

The Assassins did not take the Watch or Silver buckles. As the New Silver was only issued in the morning of the day this barbarous murder and robbery was committed, if any suspicious person put any off at public houses or shops the same evening or early the following morning, the parties who took the same are requested to give immediate information to the Mayor of Reading – and if any of the above notes have been or should be offered, the person should be immediately apprehended, the trouble and expense attending which shall be liberally remunerated, - and any person who will give information that may justify the apprehension of any persons shall be handsomely rewarded. The above sum will be paid in addition to the FORTY GUINEAS allowed by act of Parliament on conviction of the offender or offenders, by the Mayor of Reading. Reading Feb 15 1817. Several Gentlemen having entered their names to pay the above Reward, should it be called for, if any Gentleman should be inclined to increase the amount, they are requested to send their names to the Printer.

Unfortunately there is some confusion about the actual date of the murder, with some accounts giving the 12th of February. However, as the *Reading Mercury* was always published on a Monday, and the issue in which the article appears is dated the 17th, *Thursday evening* must refer to the 13th, which is the date on Longuet's memorial plaque in St James' Church. It appears that on that day he set out from Wallingford where he had collected money due to him for several months' lessons. On the way he visited friends in Pangbourne but refused their offer of overnight hospitality. The Cowslade Manuscript vividly describes their attempts to dissuade him:

The mistress of the house held a light and remarking the unusual darkness of the sky, urged him earnestly to dismount and pass the night under her roof: but assuring her that he had not the slightest apprehension, he bade her farewell and rode off at a brisk trot.

The alarm was raised when a man delivering letters found his horribly mutilated body the next morning, with the money gone and the priest's horse grazing not far away. Surprisingly his signet ring, with the royalist inscription mentioned earlier, was still on his finger. William Darter, who wrote *Reminiscences of Reading by an Octogenarian,* in 1890, remembered how, as a pupil at Reading School, he was at morning prayers when an ex-pupil arrived with the horrific news:

Our head boy, James Draper, of Theale, was reading morning prayers, when an old pupil of the Messrs. Church came into the schoolroom very much excited, and stated that he had just heard of the cruel murder of the Roman Catholic Priest (the Rev. Mr Longuet), whose body had been found with several mortal wounds in it, and was lying on the south side of the road (just beyond where now is the Barracks), and a short distance from the old turnpike, his horse being found in a narrow lane leading to the Thames.

According to Cowslade: *After the inquest, which gave no clue towards discovering the perpetrators of the murder, but showed that a sharp instrument had been used by a gash across the forehead which the cut hands had been thrown up to protect, the body was borne to the house in Vastern Lane and placed in the sanctuary of the Chapel where the members of the congregation assembled to weep and pray.*

We do not know how Bishop Poynter was brought the news but we have his own account of how he reacted. Very fortunately we have a secretary's copy of a letter he wrote to François' brother Charles, who lived in Caen. In translation the letter reads: *Please be assured that I share very deeply the grief which must be weighing on your family following the sad fate which has befallen your revered brother. As soon as I heard the news I set off for Reading where I found that the good nun, Madame Aston, had made all the preparations for his burial in his own chapel. Assisted by a number of clergy, both English and French, we recited the Office of the Dead and then I offered the Holy Sacrifice of the Mass for the repose of his soul. The people attending Mass were all weeping for the loss of their priest.*

On the 24th of February the *Reading Mercury* published a moving account of the funeral: *Wednesday afternoon the remains of the Murdered and ever to be lamented Rev. Mr Longuet, were deposited in a vault in the Catholic Chapel of this town, of which he was the Founder.*

The report includes the information that one of Longuet's last public acts had been, ironically, to help organise a meeting to congratulate the Prince Regent on his escape from attempted assassination. The paper also published part of a letter which François Longuet had sent to a Protestant clergyman in Wallingford:

This I hope, my Dear Doctor, will satisfy you as to penance; you will take all this as coming from a Catholic Man, who is sincerely convinced of the truth of his religion and bears no malice nor antipathy to those who differ from him; only I wish I could save all men and above all your nation whom I love more and more from day to day, for she is the only one, who protects oppressed justice; our King at last is forced to come and take exile among you, you have the most right to our gratitude; as to me I look upon you as one good friend and I am sincerely grateful to you, and to your nation; I would very willingly sacrifice everything to save an English person of any description; I feel a great satisfaction when I can oblige any English person, I daily pray for the prosperity of the good and generous England; may She and her children be blessed to the end of the world; I hope to give you the second article next week; and when I have done all, I intend to set at work for the Dispensary, so don't expect I shall return you so soon the sermons, for perhaps I shall find something for me in them, believe me, Dear Doctor, with respect and gratitude, your most humble and obedient servant, F. Longuet.

The reference to 'our King' must be to Louis XVIII, who ruled from 1814 until 1824 but spent part of this time in exile in England. This probably dates the letter to 1814, before his restoration, or to 1815 during Napoleon's 'Hundred Days'.

Meanwhile strenuous efforts were being made to catch the murderer and the town was clearly alive with rumours, some of which were proving highly contentious. The

Mercury's issue dated the 24th of February, among a series of articles and announcements, included the following, which appears to refer to an item published in the *Oxford Herald*. *We must, however, particularly notice, to contradict, a most unaccountable* (report), *apparently hastily invented in some Newspapers, having a tendency to reflect on the character of a most distinguished regiment, for which there is not the least truth.*

It appears that the use of a military broadsword, and witnesses' sightings of a man in what looked like a military greatcoat, had led to speculation that the murder might have been committed by a soldier. The military authorities were swift to threaten legal action if such libels were printed. On Monday March 3rd the paper reported:

The officer in command of the Royal Regiment of Horse Guards, (Blue), deems it necessary, in reference to the infamous paragraph regarding the murder of the unfortunate Mr Longuet, which appeared in the Oxford Herald, of the 21st instant, to apprise the public, that a correspondence has been opened upon the subject by the Editors of that Paper; but that the Commanding Officer not having yet received from them such a satisfactory explanation regarding the fabricators of that atrocious calumny, as he was in the first instance led to expect, proceedings are about to be instituted for bringing the authors to condign punishment.

Suspicion fell, extraordinarily, on a man with a wooden leg who had been seen leaving Pangbourne that evening. He was subsequently found to be an innocent patient returning from an appointment with a surgeon in Goring.

A subscription fund was set up, under the Mayor and the Magistrates, *to stimulate the exertions of the police and promote further enquiry.* This involved travelling expenses and the printing of posters as well as payment for *Mr Taunton from Bow Street, aided by Mr Davis of this town,* the policemen involved in the case.

The next suspect to be detained was an itinerant chair mender who had been seen with his family, who also sold rabbit skins, in the vicinity of the murder *under suspicious circumstances.* He had been wearing a coat with military buttons which he claimed to have bought from a cottager in Sulham. Attempts were also made to link him to an old military sword found in a hedge at Crowmarsh. It seems that nothing could be proved against him and he was eventually discharged in April.

We have no means of knowing what the feelings were of the owner of the *Reading Mercury*, Marianne Cowslade. Certainly everything she printed in the wake of the murder was highly eulogistic of Longuet. The following poem appeared in the edition of the 10th of March:

Adieu! Fair friendship's smile, the gen'rous heart,
    The pious Christian, unadorned by art;
Peace to thy shade! And crown'd with heavenly rest
    With Saints and Angels, may thy soul be blest!

If sacred labours claim a Christian's love,
    In deeds of charity and works above,
Thine, the cold heart, with pious thoughts inspire!
    And swell philanthropy with holy fire;
By day, by night, long years had passed with thee,
    Unceasing strive, in works of charity;
Humble thy ways, a Saviour's footsteps trod,
    And pleaded mercy, at the throne of God
For suff'ring sinners; this, to thee they owe;
    The best of blessings granted here below,
Pure was thy zeal, unmixt with bigot pride.
    A heart that ever felt, and ne'er denied
To succour sorrow, or to raise distress,
    A friend, a father to the fatherless;
Could grateful breasts, exalt thy honoured name,
    Thy merits claim the fairest wreaths of fame.

But stop! The muse must change her honest praise
    To sorrow, sadness, and to weeping lays.
If tears could speak the gen'ral burst of woe,
    Or rage terrific seize thy ruthless foe,
Thy soul, O Longuet would the living see
    With Angels' pity; look, ah! look on thee,
Behold thy wrongs! And with indignant rage,
    Proclaim revenge! Revenge! To ev'ry age.
The cruel arm, that struck the bloody blows,
    Now trembled at the deed:- no comfort knows.

Harder than steel that monster's heart must be,
    To spurn thy feeble pray'r – O pity me!
Defenceless as thou wert, no friend to save,
    And snatch thee smiling from an unwilling grave,
But thou art gone to those bright realms of light,
    Where murd'ring spirits ne'er behold the sight,
For thew his wrath a righteous God decrees!
    And stamps his mandate on their destinies,
To regions dark, where lasting torments reign,
    And endless weeping racked with bitter pain.
The guilty wretch! Now hid from mortal eyes,
    Heard murder echoed to the redd'ning skies!
The whisp'ring winds, strike terror to his soul,

And murmuring nature all his sense control.
When bloody deeds disgraced thy native land,
Britannia gave thee her protecting hand,
She soothed thy sorrow, veng'd thy injured cause,
And gave thee shelter 'neath her equal laws;
With true regret, she wails the unhappy end
Of thee! Her favoured guest and loyal friend,
Grieving she views, thy cruel wrongs and woes-
And vengeance threatens to thy barb'rous foes.

The poem is signed only F.R. It would be good to know the identity of the author.

By April the *Reading Mercury* had stopped reporting the investigation and the case seems to have gone cold. However a possible solution to the mystery appears in Darter's *Reminiscences of Reading:*

On the day this crime was committed there had been a pigeon match at Pangbourne and the supposed murderer had left the shooting party earlier than the others; but owing to his family being of such respectability and long standing in Reading, it was not until about the time of the trial of Queen Caroline (i.e. circa 1820) *that any suspicion attached to him, excepting by one or two of those in the employ of his father. No immediate attention was paid to this rumour. I, however heard from a man of the name of Rider that he had rescued the supposed murderer from committing suicide by drowning near Blake's Bridge. He soon after died, to the relief of his family.*

Darter reports that *eventually an article appeared in a local paper* deploring the fact that the supposed murderer had been sheltered by those who suspected his guilt, thereby causing great injustice to innocent people who had been arrested and investigated. He mentions that for many years after the murder there was a short inscription fixed to an elm tree near the site of the crime.

The Aftermath and the Disposal of Longuet's Property

Meanwhile Bishop Poynter had to deal with the aftermath of Longuet's death. At the end of February he received a letter from Charles Longuet, François' elder brother. In translation the letter reads: *In spite of the great grief into which the appalling death of our unfortunate brother has plunged us, we are replying as quickly as possible to your kind letter. Yes indeed, my family and I dare to claim your protection in this situation and to accept your offer of help. If anything could ease our pain it would be your generosity and the way you ministered to our unhappy brother after the tragic event which took us from him. We cannot make the journey to England and, moreover, having no knowledge of the language, the protection which you kindly offer us can help us without our being there in person.*

Longuet's friend Charles Lefèbvre, the French priest at Mapledurham, wrote to Poynter in French on the 28th of February on the delicate matter of what to do with some of Longuet's papers. The following quotations are given in translation.

There was clearly anxiety that if they got into the wrong hands they might *compromise your interests or those of our dear departed colleague.* Having gone through the letters Lefèbvre assures the Bishop that he has found some relating to the founding of the chapel, which he promises to send to London. (These are presumably the letters kept in the Westminster archive.) He is careful to state that he has told no-one that he is doing this and begs the Bishop to keep them as he, Lefèbvre, would *hate to be suspected, however unjustly, of having removed something which could be prejudicial to someone's interests, whoever that might be.*

Reading between the lines it seems likely that the family in France were demanding the return of all of Longuet's property, possibly even including the chapel furniture. This dispute was to rumble on for much of the year and Poynter must have been very glad that the deeds to the property were clearly in his name and not in that of Longuet.

Unfortunately Longuet had never made a formal will listing all his possessions since, as Lefèbvre wrote, he *was so convinced that he had done everything that was necessary to give you* (Poynter) *absolute ownership of everything concerning or belonging to the Mission which he had founded that he saw no need to draw up a will concerning it, only asking me to take note of some recommendations which he had no doubt that his family* (literally, origin) *(for whom, he thought the task of disposing of his personal effects was enough of a burden), would not wish to undertake.*

This document had been signed by his lawyer Mr Reynard, indicating some bequests as follows:

I, undersigned, by the favor of Mr Reynard, do send to my family in case of death the following sums

To my sister Rose	*£14.0.0*
= to my mother	
James' family	*£4.0.0*
Bernard's family	*£4.0.0*
Peter	*£4.0.0*
Charles	*£4.0.0*
	£30.0.0 French Louis

Amounting to English money of £33.15.0 What remains I beg of him to allow me to leave it to his children. In faith of which I sign F. Longuet

Lefèbvre regrets that Longuet never spoke to his family, when he visited them in France, about *his intentions respecting the important object which is likely now to give us so much trouble.*

It is not clear exactly to what this refers but it may in part have related to Longuet's *Missionary Library.* Apparently when asked about it by his friend Longuet had replied without hesitation: *Oh, all that goes with the Mission.* In the same letter Lefèbvre refers to a 'donation' made to Mrs Aston which seems to have caused eyebrows to be raised. He writes: *As for his donation to Mrs Aston it should not be regarded as an act of pure benevolence. Rather it is an act of justice or recognition towards a person who provided for him in his time of need, depriving herself of a comfortable living and of what he may have felt she needed now.*

Both in English and in the French original the meaning of this passage is obscure. Lefèbvre adds that he and François had both been warmly appreciative of all that this 'respectable lady' had done for Longuet.

On the envelope there is a note, dated March the 3rd, written by Poynter, or his secretary: *Things of Chapel not Mr Longuet's. Have an inventory of the rest made by an appraiser.* Unfortunately the document listing the 'things of chapel' has not survived.

On the 11th of March Poynter wrote a long and detailed letter, in French, to Charles Longuet. He starts by describing how he rushed to Reading on receiving the news of the murder. He gives details of the funeral, as earlier described, and of how he had visited *the Chief Magistrate and some other dignitaries of the town to thank them for their manifest kindness towards your brother while he was alive and most especially for their zeal in pursuing his case...*

Apart from condolences, the main purpose of the letter appears to be to convince the family that the house and chapel belonged to Church and were not Longuet's personal property: *For the rest it would appear that your brother believed that he had secured all of it for the Catholic mission of Reading, by which act he wished to make secure 'in perpetuum' the establishment itself which he had set up for this mission. I will only tell you what he himself declared to me, that it was his intention*

1.   To set up a chapel for the congregation and a house for the pastor of the Reading community.

2.   To place a sum of money into English government bonds (literally public funds) *which would yield an annual income sufficient for the livelihood of the priest, and he had planned to do all this from the fruits of his own work.*

Indeed he had saved sufficient money both to buy a moderately comfortable house and to build a chapel. To ensure that this establishment would be kept within the mission he bought it in my name. For the purpose of the second objective he had bought £300 worth of government consols at 3%, but only in his own name.

Poynter urges the family to believe what Mr Lefèbvre can tell them about their brother's intentions with regard to the library and personal possessions. It would appear that both clerics hoped that the library at least would remain in the Mission. Poynter ends by telling Charles that in any case nobody can have access to the £300 in government bonds until he, Charles, Longuet's nearest relative, authorises a lawyer to deal with the estate. The Bishop reports that he has asked a Catholic lawyer, William Talbot, (presumably a relative of the Earl of Shrewsbury), from Gray's Inn in London, to deal with the matter.

There are two letters from Mr Reynard in Reading to the Bishop, stating that he has been in communication with Mr Talbot about the details of the estate and asking for a detailed list of the property *which is to be considered as legally belonging to his family, that there may be no misunderstanding, either at the present time or hereafter.*

On the back of this letter the Bishop has written: *In consequence of the explanation which has taken place between Mr. Charles Longuet and myself it is understood that the Premises purchased in Vastern Lane, the Chapel built and whatever is contained in the chapel are excepted from the property which is to be considered as legally belonging to the family. But that the rest of his personal property, save* (or *say*) *the £300 consols with the* (unclear - possibly 'interest') *due, his movable furniture in the house, his books and clothes and whatever is due to him from any person, is claimed by his family after all his debts and funeral expenses are paid.*

This note is dated May 13th, 1817.

It is thanks to this dispute over the ownership of Longuet's property that we have the detailed description of the house and its contents as discussed earlier. It can be assumed that all of Longuet's personal effects, plus his library, were returned to the family or, more likely, that they were sold and the resulting money sent to France.

Apart from the thorny question of Longuet's property, Poynter was faced with the equally difficult problem of providing a successor to the popular priest. On the 10th of March Thomas Webster, the priest at Woolhampton, wrote to the Bishop to tell him what he proposed. Webster reported that the two French priests, Godquin and Gondré, were too elderly and frail to do more than say their existing Masses at 7 or 8 o'clock. He refers to La Noë's *unaccommodating disposition,* which would not allow him to continue much longer in saying prayers *where and at the hour he chooses.*

La Noë was in fact one of the two priests who would refuse to sign the anti-Blanchardist oath the following year and who would be banned from celebrating Mass. Webster suggests that Le Tellier (who would also refuse to sign) should say Mass at Woolhampton over the Easter period. Webster himself would go to Reading for the Holy Week services and celebrate Sunday Mass until the end of May. He also proposes to come on Saturdays to instruct the children in the chapel. Webster goes on to report the continuing *zealous activity* in the police investigation and asks what progress Poynter is making in his dealings with Longuet's family.

The only remaining letter in the archive which relates to the aftermath of Longuet's death is from Mr Hodgson, one of Poynter's Vicars General, dated the 2nd of April 1818. It relates to the withdrawing of facilities to say Mass from the Blanchardist priests, including Lanoë and Le Tellier at Reading. He goes on: *So that Reading is in a deplorable situation as the French priests are disabled by age and infirmity to say Mass, only one of them* (Godquin) *can say Mass & cannot fast beyond 8 o'clock, he is 72 years old, afflicted with the dropsy, a rupture and the other is confined to his bed or at least to his apartments. Both have signed the formula with great willingness, so have the priests at Mr Wheble* (sic) *and Mapledurham.*

The Cowslade Manuscript gives us a glimpse of life at the Reading Mission at this time:

For three ensuing years, the Reading Mission had no appointed minister. Two of the aged residents of Finch's Buildings officiated in Vastern Lane on the Sundays and Festivals, and the Rev. Webster from Woolhampton came at Indulgence times to hear confessions. The venerable Abbé Godequin (sic) *did not long continue in his share of these labours. One Sunday morning on my way to Vastern Street I met him slowly wending his way towards the Chapel, painfully dragging his legs, which were frightfully swollen with dropsy. Repelling my expressions of concern, he bade me hasten to the Chapel where he was to officiate for the last time. He secluded himself from all but priestly intercourse weeks before he was called to depart with the 'Sign of faith' and sleep the 'Sleep of peace'.*

Miss Cowslade also reports how the aged Abbé Gondré spent his time working on a translation of Duquêsne's *Evangile Médité* which was eventually published by Marianne Cowslade and sent out to the Catholic Missions in Australia.

Longuet's Legacy

While Reading's Catholics continued to worship in the Chapel of the Resurrection they would have had a constant reminder of their founder, whose body was buried, according to the *Mercury,* in a 'vault' beneath the building. No doubt many fervent prayers were said for the repose of his soul and in gratitude for his pioneering work in the town.

When St James' Church was built, as described in a later chapter, Longuet's body was moved to a place of honour at the foot of the High Altar of the new church, where a plaque still commemorates his life and tragic death.

In conclusion: what was François Longuet's legacy to the town and people of Reading?

First and foremost he gave local Catholics a Chapel for their worship and a presbytery for their priest. Secondly, by his attractive personality and openness to non-Catholics he was able to counteract many of the negative attitudes towards Catholics which had been prevalent in the town. No doubt he also persuaded many that not all Frenchmen were monsters, as propaganda might have suggested.

The reactions to his death indicate that he was held in very real affection by the townspeople of Reading.

François Longuet can rightly be regarded as the first 'parish priest' and founder of Reading's post-Reformation Catholic community.

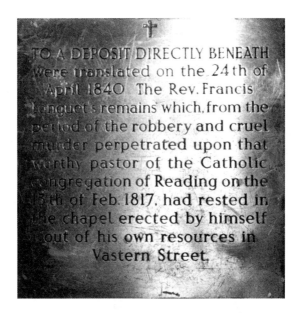

The François Longuet memorial plaque in St. James' Church.

Photograph C Widdows

PART 2

CRISIS YEARS

AND

READING'S FIRST ENGLISH PRIEST

SINCE THE REFORMATION

CHAPTER 1

CRISIS YEARS, 1817 – 1820

Introduction

Over the previous thirty years from 1787 to 1817, the Catholics of Reading had witnessed significant changes in their numbers, their status and their clergy. They had seen the days of outright persecution, clandestine meetings, and the occasional semi-legal Mass celebrated by priests such as the Franciscan, Father Baynam, based first at Whiteknights House and subsequently at Ufton Court. They had witnessed the unpleasant episode at Minster Street, followed by the security of the upper room of Finch's Buildings with its French clergy. Finally they had enjoyed the benefit of Father Longuet's purpose built Chapel of the Resurrection, with a presbytery for the priest, and a Bishop who frequently visited and cared for the Catholics of Reading.

Following Longuet's murder in 1817 the town's congregation suffered considerably. For over a quarter of a century the Catholics of Reading had relied upon French clergy, with some help from an ageing Father Baynham. Father Longuet had been a young man in his prime. Active and dynamic, he had built up good working relationships with many influential figures in Reading, transcending national and religious boundaries. He had counted many leading Protestants in Reading as his friends. During his tenure respect for the Church had grown, as had the congregation.

So what did happen at the Chapel of the Resurrection after the disastrous and sad event of February 1817? The Abbé Godquin died the next year, leaving Gondré alone, aided by Father Webster from Woolhampton, Jean Mathurin de Lanoë, until his suspension on the grounds of his Blanchardism, and the Abbé Miard de la Blardière.

The Westminster Archives hold a correspondence between an Anthony Fogg and Bishop Poynter. Fogg was a prominent local Catholic and a friend of James Wheble. Although primarily an engraver, we know from advertisements in the *Mercury* that he taught French, *having for a considerable time lived in France.* He also offered lessons in *Oil, Water Colour or Crayon.* We know that he helped in 'parish' work by giving catechism lessons.

A letter from Fogg to Poynter, dated the 27th of November 1817, shows that Fogg was closely associated with the Abbé Miard de la Blardière. Fogg was evidently handling the Chapel's accounts following Longuet's murder. He writes on behalf of Blardière requesting that Poynter should reissue the Abbé's permit to say two Masses and asks, on behalf of Blardière, whether the Bishop is coming to Reading for Confirmations. He also lists Blardière's expenses. These include the cost of a carriage for Blardière to Woodley Court:

We have often stood in need of Mr Lablardiere's (sic) *assistance as you will see by the charge of the carriage to convey him to Woodley (for he walked here) before that he walked back once or twice which was too much – One Sunday we had no Mass. Mr Gondré conceiving himself able but found himself too weak when it was too late to send to Woodley.*

We also learn from Fogg's letter that one of the Cowslade family had paid the Chapel's taxes: *May 17 To Miss* (or possibly Mrs) *Cowslade for one Quarter assessed taxes which she has paid up to midl* (sic) *1818.*

If the 'Church' was reimbursing Cowslade for taxes that she had paid then one assumes that this was because she had paid the amount from her own funds on behalf of the Church. One might surmise that this could be a property (land) tax due on Finch's Buildings which had been acquired by Elizabeth Smart (Lenoir) in 1792. Is it possible that, following the death of Longuet, the Smarts and Cowslades were managing the House in Vastern Lane?

Anthony Fogg was evidently a very prominent member of the Catholic community. He was clearly well known in Reading as an artist and a man of culture. The fact that the Bishop entrusted him with the financial affairs of the church following Longuet's death is significant in itself. In fact it is at this point that we encounter the Wheble family as connected with the Reading Mission. Taking all these factors into consideration it is reasonable to assume that he is the artist of the portrait of Blardière hanging in the Presbytery today.

Fogg reported as early as 1818 that the Abbé Gondré was not a well man. In fact he died in 1820. A radical solution was necessary.

Bishop Poynter, as we have seen from his exchange of letters with Longuet, had been intimately involved in the development of the Church in Reading. Here was a thriving community which ran the risk of losing its way. Poynter, in looking around for Longuet's replacement, chose a man who bridged the era of the French Revolution and the emerging English church. That man was Francis Bowland, whose personal life-story reflects in microcosm the wider changes taking place in the Catholic Church in England over these years. To understand his background it would be useful to take a look at where and how most English Catholic priests following the Reformation had, up to this time, received their education.

The Missionary Colleges: The English College, Douai.

In 1791 Bowland went to the English College at Douai, in Northern France, to train for the priesthood. The Bastille had been stormed, the first anti-clerical laws were being enforced, the French Revolution was already under way. But there was little evidence that events would take the dramatic turn of the next few years.

In many ways Bowland represents a last and a first, the end of one era and the beginnings of another. For over two hundred years young Englishmen had gone to Douai, Rome and Valladolid to train as priests, many of them as missionaries, risking their lives to return to England to keep the Faith alive. Francis Bowland was among the last of this cohort. He was also one of the first of the new breed of English priests to be trained and ordained in their native land.

So what was this College at Douai and why was it there?

To answer these questions we must return to the Elizabethan Settlement, the beginnings of the Penal Laws and the life of Cardinal William Allen.

Cardinal William Allen. 1532 - 1594

Had the Spanish Armada been successful, Allen's name would be as much part of English history as that of St. Thomas a Beckett or Cardinal Wolsey. Born in 1532 and a Fellow of Oriel College, Oxford, he fled England in 1561, having refused to take the Oath of Supremacy. He studied for the Priesthood at Louvain but returned to England in secret to encourage resistance to Elizabeth. He was given shelter by the Duke of Norfolk but in 1565 left England for good. In 1567 he went to Rome. Here he conceived of the plan to establish a college which would train English and Welsh priests so that, in the event of a return of Catholicism to England, the country would have a pool of trained clergy to help in the re-establishment of the Faith.

Allen returned to the Low Countries and, encouraged and helped by his Benedictine friends, he opened Douai College in 1568. The University at Douai had recently been founded by Pope Paul IV. At that time Douai was in the lands ruled by Philip II of Spain. An association between King Philip and Allen began at this point, one that was to culminate in the famous Armada.

He was joined by other English exiles fleeing Elizabethan persecution. Among these was Edward Campion. The original concept of a training ground for priests to return to a newly re-converted England, following the overthrow of Elizabeth, soon changed to one of sending missionary priests secretly to England, actively working for that change.

This ushered in one of the darkest eras in Catholic history in England. Over 150 of these missionaries were executed or martyred, with many more being imprisoned and tortured. Their presence confirmed the suspicion that the Catholic Church and certain foreign powers, especially Spain, were intent on the overthrow of the Elizabethan succession. This in turn strengthened the resolve of Elizabeth and her Parliament to pass even stronger anti-Catholic legislation.

In 1575 Allen returned to Rome and, under Gregory XIII, founded the English College, with similar aims to that of Douai. In 1578 the anti-Spanish forces, under the newly converted Protestant, William of Orange, and supported by Elizabeth, forced the College at Douai to flee to Rheims. It was here that the work of translating the Bible into English was continued. The Rheims-Douai translation of the New Testament was published in 1582. When Philip recaptured the Low Country territories the College returned to Douai. Work on translating the Bible continued and the first volume of the Old Testament was published in 1609. This English version of the Bible therefore preceded the King James' Version by two years.

It is said that Allen helped to formulate the plan to invade England and, had the Armada succeeded, he was to have been appointed Archbishop of Canterbury and Lord Chancellor. After the failure of the Spanish invasion he retired to Rome, where he died in 1594.

Catholic Education in England during Penal Times: Twyford and Old Hall Green.

In the mid 17th century, a small clandestine Catholic school was opened at Silkstead in Hampshire. It then moved to Twyford, near Winchester. The pupils were mainly young boys from well-to-do recusant families. Many progressed to more advanced studies and trained for the priesthood at one of the English Colleges mentioned above. Not all pupils, however, intended to take this course. In some cases it was merely a way to ensure that Catholic boys grew up in a Catholic environment. For example Alexander Pope was a student at Tywford but did not proceed to Douai. Twyford was closed in 1745 on account of anti-Catholic feeling caused by the Jacobite Rebellion. Bishop Challoner re-established the school at Standon Lordship, Hertfordshire, in 1749, in the grounds of a property owned by the Aston family. In 1769, Bishop James Talbot moved the school to its current site at Old Hall Green, Ware, and it became known as Old Hall Green Academy.

On the 16th of November 1793, the feast of Saint Edmund, Archbishop of Canterbury, a new College was opened. St Edmund's College was the beginning of the restoration of Catholic colleges and seminaries throughout England. Many of the boys at the school continued in the seminary and trained for the priesthood. The remaining staff and students had arrived from Douai by 1795. In the meantime students from the North had left and established a separate foundation at Ushaw College, near Durham. Gregory Stapleton was appointed as President of St Edmund's, with Poynter as his Vice President. Stapleton had been President of the English College at St Omer and, after imprisonment by the Revolutionary authorities in France, finally managed to secure the release of the last thirty-two English prisoners from Douai, celebrated as the *trente-deux*.

When Stapleton was created Vicar Apostolic of the Midland District, Poynter took over as President. Poynter had in fact been one of the *trente-deux*. In 1803, when he became coadjutor to Bishop Douglass, Poynter retained this post and held it for another ten years. Just how onerous it was to hold both these positions can be seen in the correspondence between Longuet and Poynter.

The Reverend Mr Francis Bowland

Bowland was, therefore, the first English secular priest to serve in Reading since the Reformation. Having returned to England in 1793, with the enforced closure of Douai, he completed his studies at Old Hall, where he was ordained. The Catholic Record Society archives show him officiating at Baptisms at Arundel in 1803 and 1804. He was also at Eastbourne and Petworth in Sussex. He died in 1857 at Eastbourne.

On coming to Reading in 1820 Bowland continued with Longuet's work. The congregation grew, as did the population of Reading itself. In the early 1820s Bowland added a porch to the Chapel to ease the overcrowding. The census of 1831 shows that the population of Reading was over 15,000, a threefold increase since the first census in 1801. By 1841, and with the arrival of the railway, the town's population exceeded 20,000. This period also saw a large number of Irish settling in Reading, so swelling the numbers of Catholics. At the same time the national debate over the status of Catholicism was dominated by the question of full emancipation from the old penal laws.

CHAPTER 2

Catholic Emancipation, 1829

Background

Undoubtedly the most important political movement for Catholics in the first part of the nineteenth century was the struggle for full emancipation from the remnants of the anti-Catholic penal laws.

The Acts of Union with Ireland, passed in 1800 and enacted in 1801, meant that a nation that was predominantly Catholic was now part of the United Kingdom. However Catholics were still debarred from full civic rights. Bringing Ireland fully within the Kingdom may have been astute politically in a time of war and revolution, but it created further problems.

William Pitt the Younger had envisaged Emancipation as part of the Acts of Union but George III considered that such a move would violate his Coronation Oath. In many respects he was right, but it left a political impasse that would need to be addressed. George III's Coronation Oath bound him not to do anything against the Protestant religion and he considered that granting political rights to Catholics would indeed contravene this aspect of the Oath. The conflict resulted in Pitt's resignation, as he had been unable to keep his promise to the Irish nation to incorporate Emancipation within the Acts of Union. He was replaced in 1801 by Henry Addington, First Viscount Sidmouth, who, as we have seen, had interests in Reading and had recently bought the Englefield estates, including those at Whiteknights.

Nearly all the members elected to the House of Commons after 1807 supported Emancipation. However, the House of Lords, led by George III, opposed and prevented reform.

Like the rest of the country, the town of Reading was bitterly divided over this issue. The local papers, including the Catholic-owned and edited *Mercury*, reported bitter divisions within the town. These divisions were not restricted to Protestants who opposed further relaxation of the legal restrictions on Papism. There was also discord within the Catholic community itself. We saw above that the dispute focused on the issue of the temporal power of the Papacy and its right to appoint Catholic bishops. This issue was also one of the concerns and fears of many Protestants. Any hint of a return of Papal power, let alone its influence in English law and matters of State, raised the spectres of the Jacobite rebellion, the Gunpowder Plot and two centuries of distrust of potentially subversive Catholicism.

To address these fears, in 1808, a group of influential Catholics formed the Catholic Board. To some extent this was a continuation of the Catholic Committee. Notable among its members were representatives of several leading Catholic families local to Reading: namely Michael Blount, his son Michael Henry Blount, Thomas Stonor and James Weld. All four Vicars Apostolic were members. However Bishop Milner continued in his opposition to 'lay committees' and what he saw as their English aristocratic membership. When the Board approved the principle of a State veto of candidates to bishoprics, Milner opposed this violently and left the Board in 1813. Most of the other members saw his presence as a serious obstacle to achieving emancipation.

The origins of this dispute within the Catholic Church in England can be traced back to the events examined in an earlier chapter, well before the negotiations between Pitt and the Irish Catholic hierarchy leading up to the Acts of Union. Whereas the English bishops, with the exception of Milner, were willing to negotiate on the question of the state veto on the appointment of Bishops, the Irish hierarchy, on the contrary were adamant in their opposition to what they regarded as interference in their pastoral rights and that of the Pope as Head of the Catholic Church. In an earlier chapter we saw how the members of the Cisalpine Club, led by Sir John Throckmorton, Lord Petre and Charles Butler, accepted the need for accommodation in this respect. Charles Butler, a lawyer and secretary of the Club, argued that it would be necessary *to resist any ecclesiastical interference which may militate against the freedom of English Catholics.* By this he meant interference from the Papacy.

This dispute epitomises the divisions that persisted within Catholic ranks through the first decades of the 19th century.

The 1805 Bill and its Aftermath

In 1805 Charles James Fox and Lord Grenville presented to Parliament a petition to *relieve the Irish Catholics from their civil disabilities,* in effect an Act of Emancipation. In the debate which followed, Sir John Hippisley spoke in a general way of *securities* for Catholic loyalty. That was the first time any such proposal was made in public, but nothing definite was enacted. On the 25th of May 1808 Henry Grattan, in moving for a Parliamentary Committee to consider the claims of the Catholics, said he was authorized by them to propose *that no Catholic bishop be appointed without the entire approbation of His Majesty.*

On the 27th of May Lord Grenville presented a petition for the Catholics in the Lords, proposing an effective veto for the King on the appointment of bishops. What was known as the "veto" thus assumed major significance as a public question in Ireland and in England. Whereas the majority of the English bishops were ready to accept these conditions, this was not true of the Irish hierarchy. Milner's record of events states that *both in conversation and in correspondence they universally disavowed* what had been said by the promoters of the Bill on the subject of the veto.

In 1810 Grattan gave notice that he would again bring the Catholic claims before Parliament. On the 1st of February the English Catholic Board held a meeting in London at which several resolutions were carried, including one, the 5th, which involved the veto. Charles Butler reported that *with the single exception of the Vicar Apostolic of the Midland District, agent of the Irish bishops,* (it was) *unanimously adopted.*

This 'exception' was Milner, whom the Irish bishops had engaged in 1807 to represent them in England. The Irish bishops at once condemned the 5th resolution. In May, Grattan's motion for a committee to consider the Catholic petition was defeated. Early in June, Lord Donoughmore introduced a similar motion in the House of Lords which was also defeated. This marked the parting of the ways between the great body of the Irish Catholics, led by their bishops, and the English Catholics and their bishops, with the exception of Milner.

The Gandolphy Affair and the Quarantotti Rescript.

The ill-feeling between Milner and Poynter was exacerbated by the Gandolphy affair. Father Peter Gandolphy was suspended by Poynter from his duties following publication of his sermons *in defence of the ancient faith.* Gandolphy attacked any form of 'vetoism' and was personally vindictive in published comments about Poynter. Although Poynter had suspended him from pastoral duties in his area, Milner allowed him to continue in the Midlands.

Relations between Milner and Poynter worsened after 1814 with the Quarantotti Rescript. The English Bishops, believing that a statement from Rome would assuage the fears of their Irish counterparts, successfully asked for, and duly received, a letter from Monsignor Quarantotti, Secretary of the *Sacra Congregatio de Propaganda Fide* (the Sacred Congregation for the Propagation of the Faith) in which he stated that it would be allowable for a veto to be part of an Act of Emancipation, so long as this did not go so far as to give power of appointment to the English Crown. Far from being assuaged, the Irish Bishops and Milner made direct representations to Pope Pius VII, who had been a prisoner of Napoleon when the Rescript was issued. The Pope retracted Quarantotti's statement and instigated instead an enquiry into the whole matter.

The affair, if not fully resolved, was settled by 1815 when the Vatican issued a statement, supported by the Pope, from Cardinal Litta of Propaganda Fide. It stated that, as part of any Act of Emancipation, the British Government's desire to examine letters between the Catholic bishops and the Holy See *cannot even be taken into consideration.*

With regards to the 'veto' it said that quite enough provision had been made for the loyalty of candidates in the Catholic oath. However, for their greater satisfaction, it permitted *those to whom it appertains* to present to the King's ministers a list of the candidates selected for bishoprics. It insisted that if those names were presented the Government must, if it should think any of them *obnoxious or suspected,* name them *at once.* Moreover a sufficient number, from amongst whom the Pope would appoint the bishop, must always remain even after any government objection.

The Irish bishops sent deputies to Rome to make known their feelings to the Pope. Two replies were sent, one to the bishops and the other to the laity. The Pope insisted on the terms of Cardinal Litta's letter, pointing out its reasonableness under the circumstances. According to the terms of the letter it would, in fact, be the fault of the ecclesiastics who made the selection of candidates if any undesirable person were left for Papal appointment. Cardinal Litta's letter was the last Papal document issued on the veto question. The controversy between *vetoists* and *anti-vetoists* had, however, aroused deep passions and ill feelings continued on both sides.

In 1821 the Earl of Fingall put forward proposals for Catholic emancipation. This included power of veto for the government on nominees for Catholic bishoprics and a modification to the Oath of Supremacy. Bishop Milner, Vicar Apostolic of the Midland District, (who had been a baptismal sponsor to the Whebles at Woodley Lodge the previous year) opposed the bill. However, the Vatican and Bishop Poynter supported it with reservations. The bill was subsequently passed by the House of Commons but rejected by the Lords.

Reading in 1820

If there was turmoil throughout England over this issue, this was reflected in Reading, which had its own troubles. Newspaper reports and letters to the *Mercury* show ever-increasing divisions in the townsfolk. Miss Cowslade, one of the daughters of Thomas Cowslade and Marianne Smart, in her account written most probably in 1841, several times refers to the hostility that Catholics faced in the town. There is one poignant passage where she notes how Catholic schoolchildren had previously been bullied by their fellows. Following the opening of the new Church in 1841 she rejoices that *Catholic children can now go to their own Church or school without being hooted by a youthful rabble.*

There are several exchanges of correspondence in the *Mercury* between concerned Protestants and leading Catholics such as Michael Blount and Sir John Throckmorton. These, and others, frequently wrote to reassure the citizens of Reading about Emancipation but quite vitriolic opposition continued for many years. It would appear that the days when François Longuet could work with his Protestant colleagues in raising money for the Town Dispensary were in the past.

PART 3

ST JAMES' CHURCH

CHAPTER 1

THE WHEBLE FAMILY

AND THE BUILDING OF ST JAMES' CHURCH

The Wheble Family

James Wheble: Illustration hanging in the presbytery of St James'.

Just as the Smart family had been major players in bringing Catholic worship back to Reading in the latter part of the eighteenth century, so the name of Wheble dominates the middle part of the nineteenth.

The portrait shown presents a significant challenge. It is not clear whether it depicts the elder James Wheble (c.1729 - 1801) or his son, also James, (1779 - 1840). There are good arguments to support either view. We have consulted several art critics, including one from the National Portrait Gallery, which also has a copy, and another who is an expert in this period. The consensus is that the portrait is of a youngish man posing in dress consistent with that worn at the end of the 18th century. This would indicate that the picture portrays the younger James, founder of St. James', possibly at the time of his marriage in 1802.

The elder James Wheble, who founded the Kensington Candle Manufactory, was worth at least £200,000 at his death. In his will he bequeathed a personal fortune of £150,000 to his wife Jane. In addition to this he left £50,000 to the Reverend John Milner, later Bishop Milner, for the use of the Winchester Catholic congregation, and possibly a further £150,000 to his son James. The will is difficult to decipher and it may be that reference is being made to the same £150,000, left first to his widow and then to his son on reaching the age of majority. Elsewhere there is a claim that James Wheble left £200,000. Whatever the total value of his estate, it constituted a considerable fortune.

James was a member of a recusant family in Winchester. He had connections with the Arundell family; one record indicates that he had once been 'butler to Lady Arundell'. We also know that his father, Richard, bought Woodley Lodge in about 1760. It would appear that a Matthew Berry first acquired this in trust for Richard. The exact identity of Matthew Berry and his relationship with Richard remain unclear.

The evidence points to James inheriting Woodley Lodge in 1771 from his father. He built a new house after about six years but sold the estate to Henry Addington in 1789. Addington, later Viscount Sidmouth, on becoming Prime Minister in 1801, sold the house back to the younger James Wheble. According to a document in the Berkshire Records' Office, James paid £27,000 for the property.

Woodley Lodge in the late 19th century
Courtesy of Reading Library

We do know that by 1766 the elder James Wheble was living in Kensington Square, and over the next few years his business prospered. He occupied several properties on and behind the present 'Barkers' site, both in Kensington High Street and on the west side of Young Street. From 1772 onwards a warehouse was rated here in his name. In

1779, on the sale of a certain Samuel Walsh's freeholds, Wheble bought Nos. 34, 36 and 37, Kensington Square, along with several houses in the section of the High Street west of King (now Derry) Street. He lived at No. 36 until his death in 1801.

Kensington Square: No. 34, with the blue door. No. 36 to the right behind the tree.

The Whebles, as well as being exceptionally wealthy, were also 'well connected' in Catholic circles. The younger James was acquainted with the Talbot family, including the Earl of Shrewsbury. In 1802 he married Maria Talbot, niece of the 14th Earl. Her nephew, Bertram Arthur, son of her brother Lt. Col. Charles Thomas, later became the 17th Earl.

We are fortunate in having a written account of the courtship of James and Maria Talbot.

In July 1802 Charles Dormer, a relative of the Talbot family, describes *Mr. Wheble's admiration for Miss Talbot and his efforts to obtain her society.* He goes on to say: *Apparently the whole family is plotting their future marriage.* He further talks about a *lovers' tiff between Mr. Wheble and Miss Talbot. She will not give him a final answer yet, but the outcome is likely to be an affirmative.*

By the 10th of September news has spread *of Mr. Wheble's engagement to Miss Talbot, settling £1000 p.a. on her with £200 pin money...*

They were married on the 22nd of September 1802. On the 3rd of November William Talbot reports that he has received news of his sister's marriage to Mr. Wheble and by May 18th 1803 he writes saying he hopes he will be able to call and see his sister at Woodley.

Once settled at Woodley Lodge, James and Maria soon started their family. Some reports say that his mother, Jane, initially went to live in the Milner Household in

Wolverhampton. However it is possible that she moved back to Reading and the new family seat at Woodley, for according to the Woodley Lodge Registers she died there in 1839 at the age of 89. Over the next ten years James and Maria had five children, all girls. Their first child, Maria Joanna (the Woodley Lodge Registers are in Latin) and may have been called Maria Jane or Mary Jane, was baptised on the 7th of July 1803. The sponsors were Francis Talbot, Maria's father, and Jane Wheble, James' mother. The register is signed *P. La Blardière.*

Abbé Pierre Louis Guy Miard de la Blardière

Oil portrait of Abbé Miard de la Blardière © St James' Parish, Reading

We saw in an earlier chapter that Abbé Miard de la Blardière was one of the first four priests to arrive in Reading in 1793 and that he was resident at Finch's Buildings. In 1802 he moved from Finch's Buildings to become chaplain to the Wheble family. James Wheble's first chaplain was William Allan of Isleworth. It would appear that Father Allan waited to see whether the French priest could indeed cope with the duties of domestic chaplain. Having satisfied himself, and now doubt James Wheble, that this was the case, he returned to Isleworth. James Wheble provided Blardière with a house in the grounds of the Lodge. This was within easy reach of the mansion where the Abbé said Mass every morning. On Sundays he celebrated Mass and officiated at other services for the family and locals.

If we are inclined to believe that life was easy for James Wheble and his aristocratic wife, then even at this distance of 200 years, we cannot but share the pain that must have been felt in the household when, on the 25th of January, 1814, tragedy struck. Maria died, leaving James widowed with five daughters, the youngest only two years of age. Maria was buried in the Catholic Cemetery, Winchester. We can also only imagine the role their Chaplain played at this time. However the baptismal records from the Lodge for 1815, a year after Maria's death, show that 'James and Maria' are sponsors at a baptism. The next year they have a child called Maria Juliana. The explanation is that James married again very soon after his first wife's death. His new wife was also called Maria and the Register shows that her maiden name was O'Brien.

In 1817, on the 29th of June, James Joseph was baptised. This was James' first male child. Over the next twelve years James and Maria had a further seven children, making a total from his second marriage of nine children. In addition there were the five from his first marriage. In the baptismal records we read that on the 28th of November 1824 Bishop Milner was at the Lodge and was baptismal sponsor to John Joseph. In April 1829 the Whebles entertained another distinguished guest at a Baptism: Daniel O'Connell. This was just two weeks after the passing of the Catholic Emancipation Act. The child's baptismal name is given as Daniel O'Connell and the great Irishman, who had been so instrumental in having the Emancipation Act passed, was his godfather.

The Wheble household was not without further tragedies. Apart from the loss of his first wife, James was to suffer many more bereavements. In 1824 he lost two children in a fire on the same day: Frances Margaret, aged 19, and Maria Theresa aged only 4. The Whebles then lost another four children over the next eight years. The death of his mother, aged 89, in 1839, though doubtless a sad event, would have been expected but came after the death of his second wife in 1834. He himself died at the age of 61 on the 20th of July 1840.

We know that Blardière was chaplain to the Wheble household up to at least 1833 or 1834. This date is based upon the Baptismal Records of Woodley Lodge which show that in November 1833 his name is replaced by that of the Reverend John Ringrose. However, according to Miss Cowslade, Blardière only returned to France much later. She writes: *He carried on till the foundation of the Church on the site of the ruins of Reading Abbey, an event which for years he had ardently desired.*

Since the building of St James' Church started in 1837 and lasted until 1840, it is possible that Blardière stayed on after he was no longer the official chaplain. According to Cowslade: *he then retired to Rouen to close his priestly career where it had begun, bequeathing, when called to his reward, his own chalice to the Church of St James, for which, when he had purchased it, he intended this memorial.* The chalice is still in the possession of the parish. It has a Paris silver mark and can be dated to between 1819 and 1838.

Abbé Miard de la Blardière's Chalice   © St James' Parish, Reading

We hear nothing from Blardière himself. We have some written records from most of the other protagonists but nothing from him. However, as chaplain to the Wheble household, as tutor to James' children, as confidant to one of the most influential of Catholic families in the Reading area, his influence must have been considerable.

The Abbey Ruins and James Wheble

1829 was the year of the Catholic Emancipation Act which, among other reforms, allowed Catholics to hold Offices of State. James, already a well-known figure around Reading area, entered more into public life. He was well regarded and was known as a benefactor to Catholics and Protestants alike, donating, for instance, money to Protestant Churches.

He was closely involved in the complicated negotiations between the owner of much of the Abbey Ruins, Mr. Vansittart (Lord Bexley as of 1833), and prominent members of the town, including the Mayor. Despite a public subscription, and the successful acquisition by a trust of some of the ruins, the most important areas, including the cloister, the south and north transepts and the nave, remained the property of Lord Bexley. In 1834 Wheble bought these areas from Lord Bexley including what was to become the eastern end of the Forbury Gardens.

Perhaps the death of James' second wife in 1834 played a role in his determination to excavate the remains of the old Abbey. Some of the fruits of his excavations can be seen in the fabric of the present Church and Presbytery, as well as in the wall now separating the Forbury Gardens from St James'. Not least in importance is the Church's baptismal font, constructed from one of the capitals unearthed by Wheble in his excavations of the cloister area in the Abbey ruins.

It is unknown at what point Wheble set in motion his plans to build a Church and a presbytery on his newly acquired land. We do know that there was a perceived need to provide a larger chapel for the growing Catholic population in and around Reading. Father Bowland had been raising money for a new or extended Chapel from at least 1830.

It seems likely that once he had acquired the Abbey lands James, at some point, decided that this would be an ideal spot for the new church. Any problem about its location was solved. Moreover financing the new building was no longer an issue, as Wheble was content to provide the money. He chose the area adjacent to the North Transept of the ruined Abbey for the church and sacristy, with the presbytery being built just south of this point.

It is possible that James decided to build his church just outside the line of the transept because he wished to continue his excavations, especially in the cloister. However these plans were brought to an end by his death in 1840.

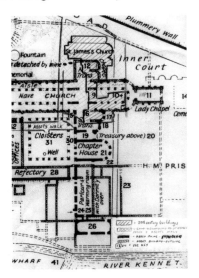

The plan shows in outline the footprint of the old Abbey. The hatched area shows existing buildings, mostly dating to the 19th century.   Courtesy Reading Museum and J Mullaney

His son and heir, James Joseph, sold the cloister area to a local builder who in turn sold this on to John Weedon, a Reading solicitor. The latter also bought, from James Joseph in 1844, the strip of land to the west of the cloister which became today's Abbot's Walk.

The First Priest in Charge of St James' Church

There has been some debate as to why Francis Bowland did not take over at St. James'. Miss Cowslade says that on *finding he was not to be appointed he retired and was succeeded by Father Thomas Mylius Molteno.*

The annual returns to London from the Vastern Street Chapel show a consistent attendance from 1834 to 1836 of about 70 people. We also know that Bowland was raising money for a new Chapel over this period. So why was he not offered the post? It was claimed at the time, a claim repeated in subsequent accounts, that James Wheble wanted the renowned cleric Dr Daniel Rock to take over the post. The origin of this assertion comes from the Cowslade manuscript where Miss Cowslade states that: *It had been the fixed intention of Mr Wheble, when the church which he had founded and was then erecting should be completed, to obtain the appointment of the above-mentioned* (Dr. Rock*) distinguished ecclesiastic to its ministry.*

Miss Cowslade goes further: *But Dr. Rock was resolute in his refusal and the unlooked for disappointment conveyed a shock to Mr Wheble, which, suffering as he then was from disease of the heart, was thought to be the immediate cause of his sudden death.*

Dr. Rock was the chaplain and friend of the Earl of Shrewsbury. In 1836 he was 37 years old, a renowned scholar of the Old Catholic tradition, a believer in the power of architecture and art as expressions, or outwards signs, of the spiritual reality of the 'sacred mysteries' of the Mass. He was also interested in promoting the use of the Sarum Rite, the ritual widely used in pre-Reformation England.

It is not surprising that Rock, on reading Pugin's work *Contrasts* (published in 1836), discovered a kindred spirit and promoted the young architect's interests, not least with the Earl of Shrewsbury. It should be remembered that this coincided with the early days of the Tractarian Movement, so called after the 90 *Tracts for the Times,* which sought to affirm the Catholic tradition within the Church of England. John Henry Newman wrote the first of these tracts in 1833. Newman famously later converted to Rome in 1845, having written the last Tract, number 90.

The connections between James Wheble and Shrewsbury, and his evident friendshipwith Bishop Milner, indicate that Wheble would have preferred a new face in his new church. Francis Bowland had been Bishop Poynter's appointee, indeed had been one of his students in Douai. We know that Poynter and Milner had been in deep disagreement over the future shape of the Church in England. It is reasonable to assume that James Wheble was more sympathetic to Shrewsbury's and Rock's vision of the future Church. Employing Pugin, the leading architect who was promoting these ideas, was therefore also a logical move.

However Dr Rock declined the post. He did briefly hold the position in July 1840 before becoming chaplain to Sir Robert Throckmorton of Buckland. Dr Rock was an academic, and evidently wished to devote time to his studies rather than to parish business. From 1837 to 1840, therefore, Father Molteno was in charge of the Vastern Street Chapel of the Resurrection while St. James' was being built.

There is a letter in the Westminster Archives from James Wheble which throws a very different light on the affair. On the 5th of January 1840 he wrote a very strong, and one might say angry, letter to Bishop Griffiths, Vicar Apostolic for the London area, concerning the question of the appointment of a Priest to St James' Church. Wheble writes about *the annoyance and great misfortune now in store for me partly through your Lordship's indecision respecting the appointment of a clergyman to the Reading Mission. You know full well that I pressed for no one, and asked for no one, but rumours and hints led me and others to believe that Mr ?* (presumably Ringrose - unfortunately the writing is indistinct at this point) *was certainly to be the person.*

The story that James Wheble was the reason for Bowland's departure must be reconsidered. It would seem from this letter that the initiative came from the Bishop and it was only after Bowland's departure that Wheble expressed any preference. Taking Wheble at his word, even this is debatable, he claims in a private letter to have no preference. It also casts doubt on Miss Cowslade's assertion that Dr Rock's refusal to take up a permanent position was the cause of James' untimely death.

We saw above that John Ringrose took over signing the Woodley registers in 1833 and that there may be some doubt as to whether Blardière was still at the Lodge. Whatever the case, Ringrose became the first permanent priest of St James' Church in 1840. He was certainly there in August 1840, shortly after the Church was officially opened, as we have a letter from Pugin addressed to him dated the 22nd of August. This is reproduced in full in Appendix E and clearly demonstrates Pugin's close interest in St James' even whilst he was engaged in many other projects. It has been claimed that Pugin wished to distance himself from St James', his only design in Norman Romanesque style in England. The passion of this letter to Ringrose would indicate otherwise, but this is a topic I shall look at in greater detail in a subsequent chapter.

CHAPTER 2

Pugin's First Church Design.

The Building and Opening of St James' Church.

Laying the Foundation Stone, 1837

In 1837 James Wheble became Sheriff of Berkshire. The *London Gazette* printed the following report:

At the Court at Brighton, the 28th day of January 1837, The KING'S Most Excellent Majesty in Council. SHERIFFS appointed by His Majesty in Council, for the Year 1837. Berkshire: James Wheble, of Woodley-Lodge, Esq.

Miss Cowslade marks the moment by recording *the nomination of James Wheble to the office of High Sheriff of the County and his, so to speak, triumphal entrance into the town on the first day of the Assizes with an escort of Gentry and Yeomanry unprecedented in number and importance on any former occasion. The Catholic Sheriff, loyal to his Faith, and outspoken in its profession, went in his carriage with his domestic Chaplain by his side and his retinue preceding and following him, to the obscure Lane and humble Chapel which had never till then witnessed such a gathering. The Catholics in the town then first began to hold up their diminished heads.*

By the time this momentous event took place, plans were already being made for a replacement to the 'humble Chapel'. Having acquired the land and engaged Pugin as his architect, on the 14th of December 1837 Wheble ended this year with another spectacular and historically important event, the first public Catholic service in Reading since the Reformation: the laying of the foundation stone of the new church.

According to a contemporary newspaper report, thirteen carriages were required to bring the party from Bulmershe (Woodley Lodge) to Reading. Alongside James Wheble and the Catholic gentry came the Bishop with sixteen of his clergy. As for the procession itself, the ritual of the Roman Catholic Church certainly seems to have caught the public eye. In a long article the *Mercury* reported:

First came the cross bearer in a white alb and a beautifully embroidered dalmatic; on each side of the cross walked two acolytes clothed in white surplices and handsome purple cassocks faced with crimson... The clergy came next... and lastly the Bishop in a splendid mitre and beautifully ornamental vestments and bearing in his right hand an elegantly wrought cross.

The sermon, given by Father James O'Neil, was heard in the *greatest silence* by between two and three thousand people. It was followed by the singing of Psalms 83, 126, 50, 86 and 121. It was reported that *the chant of the Miserere was particularly beautiful,* after which the Bishop, *assisted by Mr Welby Pugin, the architect,* laid the first stone of the building. The service was concluded with the singing of the *Te Deum.*

Pugin and the Norman-Romanesque Style

The fact that Pugin agreed to design the church in the Norman Romanesque style is surprising considering his entrenched views about the 'correct style' for a Christian church, namely what we now refer to as neo-Gothic. This has generated much debate, some of it even casting doubt on Pugin's role and interest in the building. Indeed it is a fact that was commented on in contemporary records. *The Tablet,* in reporting the event, stated that: *Every external part of the edifice is in strict accordance with the spirit and style of the architecture of the age to which it refers; and whatever difference of opinion may be allowed of different styles, there can be none in the decision that no other style would have been appropriate to the sacred spot on which it stands.* This appears to have been, and has remained, the prevailing opinion and explanation as to why Pugin, such a vociferous advocate of the neo-Gothic, agreed to design a church in the Norman Romanesque style. It is most likely that Wheble wanted his new church, to be in the same architectural style as Reading's ruined Abbey.

In early 1838 William Fletcher published a book, *Reading, Past and Present,* in which there appears a print of St James' Church. See figure 1. The wording is as follows: *A. Welby Pugin is the Architect, and we have been favoured with the opportunity of supplying our readers with a sketch of the Church, by James Wheble, Esq. of Woodley Lodge.* It is an interesting sketch, as it appears to show the finished church, whereas at the time of its execution, 1837 or 1838, it is unlikely that the building was so far advanced. It is, however, a remarkably accurate representation of the final building and one might be excused for surmising that Pugin himself had a hand in its production. The drawing is signed *Fletcher del.* This indicates that Fletcher was the artist, 'del' being the abbreviation for 'delineate' or 'drawn by'. Fletcher does also give some attribution to Wheble. Could it be that Wheble allowed Fletcher to see Pugin's plans from which he composed the picture we now see?

There are certain elements of this print that merit closer examination. First of all the tower in the background to the right is that of St Lawrence's Church. On the far left can be seen the Abbey Ruins. As for the structure itself, the west end gable kneeler is missing. A kneeler is the architectural term for the stones on which the gable-end coping rests. The illustration of the completed church shown in figure 2, possibly by Marianna Frederica Cowslade, clearly shows its presence

The stonework around the apse appears to reach to the ground whereas the evidence we have from the existing structure, now inside the church but originally on the outside, is that the facing was of flint below the gable, matching the body of the nave and frontage. It also appears that the stringcourses, which are a continuation of the window dripstones and which tie into the buttresses, are missing.

A couple of the windows appear to have pointed arches. The cross on top of the bellcote is out of proportion. Today the cross at the west end is no longer there though there are later photographs, even as late as the 1950s, which show it in position and in proportion. Most significant of all is the buttress at the northeast angle. The existing building has a much wider and deeper buttress than shown in Fletcher's book. Early photographs and even earlier sketches indicate that the church was built with this 'double' buttress. It seems a fair conclusion to say that the drawing was an artistic impression of what the church would look like but that alterations or refinements were made at the time of building.

I referred above to another sketch of the church, possibly by Marianna Frederica Cowslade. This can be found in a volume of drawings held in Reading Library. The catalogue date is given as 1833. This is not possible since the Church was not even planned until 1836 to 1837. Moreover if one looks closely it is possible to spot an early steam locomotive in the distance and the railway only came to Reading in 1840.

The volume is ascribed to Marianna Frederica but this may be because her name appears on the first page and it could indicate that the book merely belonged to her. Whatever its provenance, the sketch is interesting in showing not just the Church but also one of the very few contemporary images of the adjoining Presbytery. Marianna (sometimes spelt Marianah) Frederica Cowslade was the daughter of Frederic Cowslade and Anne Walpole. As we have seen, Frederic became joint owner of the *Mercury* with his brother Henry. At the time of the 1841 Census the family lived at 6 Market Place, the site of the *Mercury* offices. Marianna Frederica had two brothers: John who joined the Indian army and William Wallace who inherited the family business and lived until 1915.

In 1850 Marianna married Richard Edward Dent (born Rippon). He had changed his name to Dent when his stepfather, Edward John Dent, married his widowed mother, Elizabeth. Marianna Frederica found herself joint proprietor of the well-established and famous clock makers, EJ Dent & Co. This company had been given the contract to supply the clock for the new Houses of Parliament. On the death of her father-in-law, Marianna set up a separate branch of the firm: MF Dent. Despite legal wrangling and opposition from within the Parliamentary committee, the clock we now know as Big Ben was finally installed in 1859.

The Official Opening of St James 1840

The building of St James' Church appears to have met with several problems. One, which I shall not discuss in depth, but which should be mentioned, was opposition from some townsfolk. It centred on the question of the right of way which cut across the grounds where the Church was being built. Whether the outcry stemmed from anti-Catholic feeling or was a justifiable grievance is hard at this distance in time to judge. It was probably a combination of the two. There is copious correspondence in the local press over this issue. The Cowslade Manuscript hints at other problems, citing: *the vexatious obstacles and delays which had prolonged the erection of the new building.* Unfortunately Miss Cowslade is not specific in giving details. If we remember that the Foundation stone was laid in late 1837, and the Church was operational by August 1840, we may think that thirty-two months is not, in fact, an unreasonable time.

Pugin was the designer of the building. He had converted to Catholicism in 1835 and was the most prominent Catholic architect of his day. The directory of British Listed Buildings says that St James' was Pugin's first church design. As seen above, he was present at the ceremony of laying the first stone. This was at the *southern angle* of the building. Unfortunately researches to date have failed to locate it. It was possibly moved or built over during the 1926 extensions. It is clear that despite being engaged in designing several churches in Wexford, Ireland, and others in England, not least the building of a new Catholic Church (later Cathedral) of St Chad's, Birmingham, Pugin kept an eye on proceedings in Reading. His visit to Reading in August 1840 is documented in his own letter, which refers to his contact with James Wheble and to *furnishing him with drawings for an entrance gateway & a stone cross to stand in* (the*) cemetery.*

The Church was opened in August 1840. The occasion was not however the joyous, celebratory event that had been planned by James Wheble. Arrangements had been made that the Church should be officially opened on the 5th of August, the Feast of the Blessed Virgin *ad Nives,* or Our Lady of the Snows. In the event James Wheble died of a heart attack on the 20th of July, within three weeks of the proposed ceremony. The *Reading Mercury* reported his death in its issue of the 27th of July, commenting on his being *a true Christian with no regard to Sects* whose *purse was open to all Catholics, Protestants and Dissenters.* On the 1st of August the paper reported on his funeral procession in the following words:

On Tuesday morning last the remains of James Wheble were conveyed from Woodley lodge to the Catholic Burying Ground at Winchester to be deposited in the family vault. The sad procession left the mansion at half past eight o'clock; the mourning coaches contained five sons of the deceased, and those clerical and other gentleman who particularly shared his friendship and confidence. The cortège was joined for some miles by the carriages of all the leading gentleman of Reading and of the neighbourhood for many miles round, forming altogether a good and solemn spectacle, and offering a last tribute to the memory of one who will be long and deservedly regretted.

At Winchester, the funeral procession was met by other carriages in which were several clerical gentlemen, friends and relatives of the deceased. The burial service was performed by the Rev. --- Delaney of Winchester. The tomb closed over the mortal remains amid the deep and heartfelt sorrow of the numerous assemblage. Never were outward demonstrations of respect evinced by truer mourners. To those who have to lament the sudden and irreparable loss of such a person and such a friend it must be consoling to receive clear proofs of almost universal sympathy and to cherish the recollection of a life whose constant aim was to give glory to God and show goodwill to men.

In spite of this tragedy it was decided to proceed with the opening as scheduled. Miss Cowslade wrote that the service *was executed to the letter, by the Bishop and Clergy of the Diocese, who, with closed doors, consecrated the building on that day.* The *Tablet,* a few days later, also reported the event. Both accounts refer to the unkind comments by some Reading people about the inscriptions on the Baptismal font. As mentioned above, James Wheble, during his excavations of the ruins, had discovered this piece of masonry which is probably a capital from the old Abbey cloister. Anticipating the opening ceremony, Wheble commissioned a pair of brass plates to be attached to the two worn surfaces of the stonework. These are still present and can be seen on the baptismal font which now stands at the East end of the North aisle of the Church. The inscription reads: *The foundation stone of St. James's Church was laid Dec. 14, 1837, and Divine Service was first performed therein on the Feast of the B.V. ad Nives, Aug 5, 1840.*

Miss Cowslade merely writes: *Comments, especially painful to Catholics' ears were consequent upon this premature inscription.* The *Tablet* gives a fuller report: *Comments and moralisms have not been spared in certain classes on the temerity of recording, as past, events that are to come. But those who do not confound the anxious zeal of a good Christian, in a holy cause with the vain glory of mere human ambition, are inclined to regard this inscription, piously borne out as it has been, rather as prophetic than as presumptuous.* (See Appendix D for a full transcription of the article from the *Tablet*). It should be noted that 1840 was also the foundation year of this prestigious Catholic paper.

The opening service of consecration was low key, in memory of its founder and in consideration for his mourning family. The *Tablet* commented that: *On the following Sunday, the sound of their own church bell, a new sound to the Catholic inhabitants of Reading, was hailed by them with mingled grief and gratitude, and assembled them all under the stately roof of the newly completed building.*

In fact the building was not totally completed. As mentioned above, Pugin visited the Church in late August and wrote a letter, postmarked the 22nd, to Father Ringrose, listing ten items which required urgent attention. Amongst these was the decoration of the Altar and of the Chancel, (cf Appendix E). On the 28th of November, Bishop Griffiths returned to Reading and consecrated the High Altar.

In 1840, on the 10th of March, James Wheble had written a will by which *the above land, Church and other buildings* came into the possession of his son James Joseph Wheble who *desired* to convey them to the Church authorities. Consequently an agreement was drawn up in March 1841 between Bishop Thomas Griffiths (Vicar Apostolic, London), and James Joseph Wheble, that the *Church and other buildings be conveyed* to the Church. The final act in the founding of the new church of St James and the closure of the Chapel of the Resurrection is to be found in a document from the Registrar of Reading, dated the 13th of September 1841, which states that St James' Church *was substituted for the registered building now disused, named Vastern Street Chapel.* According to the 1851 Census there was accommodation in St. James' for two hundred and sixty two people, whist an Ordnance Survey map for 1875 puts the figure at two hundred and seventy eight.

PART 4

PUGIN

AND

THE DESIGN OF ST JAMES' CHURCH

CHAPTER 1

The Question about the Original Design

The Abbey Ruins

There had been a number of drawings, etchings and engravings made of the Abbey Ruins during the 18th century. Most contained inaccuracies or were written in a spirit of early Romantic sentiment rather than with any concern for archaeological or historical accuracy. In 1776 Sir Francis Englefield undertook a more scientific survey of the Ruins. He was an antiquarian of some note and, as we have seen, played a significant role in the return of Catholicism to England and to Reading. His paper was published in the journal *Archaeologia* and contains accurate sketches and descriptions of the Ruins. He gives the dimensions of the Abbey buildings but is careful to say where these are estimates. For a fuller analysis of this work see Dr. Cecil Slade's book *The Town of Reading and its Abbey.*

In the preceding chapter we looked at James Wheble's interest in, and purchase of, the Abbey Ruins. It would appear that James wanted the new church to be a sign of the re-establishment of Catholicism on the *sacred site* of the old Abbey. Not only was his new Church to be built in the Norman Romanesque style, reminiscent of the Abbey, but its name was to be St. James', recalling the ancient Abbey's dedication to that saint, a name which coincided with his own, his father's and that of his eldest son.

According to one contemporary newspaper account, the Church was constructed, *as far as the mason's art allowed,* with flint and stone from the old Abbey. Apart from the use of these materials to build the Church, there is still evidence of other remnants from these excavations in the walls of the Church and Presbytery and in the wall separating the Forbury Gardens from St James'.

The main 'find' was the column capital which Wheble had converted into a Baptismal font and which still stands in the Church, though not in its original position. At the time there was some speculation as to the nature or purpose of this intricately carved block of oolitic limestone. One likely explanation is that it is the remains of a carved capital from the columns of the cloister of the old Abbey.

As the following late 19th century photograph shows, the font was originally placed at the entrance to the Church, set on tiles which look very much as if they too had been excavated from the Abbey Ruins. One in particular has the appearance of a medieval encaustic tile, namely a fired tile with an inlaid pattern.

Fig 1 The font in its original position

Another detail to note from this photograph is that we can make out two doors, a large one directly behind the font and a smaller one to its right, with a holy water stoup in between. One assumes that to maintain symmetry there would have been a third door to the left. But these are not outside doors.

If we look at photographs of the exterior of the church (figs. 2 and 3) we see that the original frontage had only one main entrance. It was this that was moved forward by Mangan in 1926. The whole of the interior wall, with its three doors and two holy water stoups, was then placed in the position of the original outside wall. Standing inside the main body of the church today, one can see a cased beam stretching the width of the nave supporting the choir loft. It is reasonable to assume this was the position of the interior entrance to the church.

Fig 2   Fig 3

Photographs courtesy of St James' Church

If these assumptions are correct there was in fact a narthex, or entrance area, the width of the church and 10' deep, with three doors giving access to the nave where the font was placed. The narthex is just about discernible in Fig 3.

The Norman Romanesque Style

Returning to the question about the overall original design, there have been many comments made to the effect that St James' is Pugin's only church, in England, in the Norman Romanesque style. In fact Pugin employed this style on only three occasions: at St James', for the crypt of St Chad's Church, (later Cathedral) in Birmingham, and for the church of St Michael the Archangel in Gorey, Co. Wexford, in Ireland.

Almost without exception, commentaries about Pugin refer to his dictum that the only true form of Christian architecture was the 'pointed' style. It seems surprising, therefore, that he should agree to undertake a commission employing Norman Romanesque features. Although the explanation may lie, as seen, in the new Church being built in homage to the old Abbey, perhaps we should look deeper and examine what Pugin did, as opposed to what he wrote.

In works such as his *Apology,* Pugin stresses the need for consistency of style and that design should flow from the nature of the building and not be imposed by some preconceived foible of the architect or patron. Pugin might well have justified his design for St. James' on the basis that he was being consistent with the style of the period for which he was designing; hence a Norman style to reflect a Norman Abbey. Wheble's association with the Talbot family and the Earl of Shrewsbury, alongside his acquaintance with Dr Rock, may have been another incentive for Pugin to bend to James' preferences. For an architect who had not to that date built a church, these were indeed powerful and influential people, whose patronage must have demanded serious consideration.

St James' was Pugin's first church design and, although he does not follow his dictum about the 'pointed style', it is arguable that he did not in fact abandon his architectural principles. Following the publication of *Contrasts,* which attracted the attention of Dr Rock, Pugin worked on his theory about the principles of Christian architecture. These are famously contained in his lectures delivered at Oscott in 1841 and published under the title *The True Principles of Pointed or Christian Architecture.* Remembering that Pugin at this early stage of his career was still developing and refining his ideas, it is possible, in examining the details of St James', to discern how many of the principles are in fact embedded in the design.

Pugin was a complex character, as reflected in his writings. His views and opinions altered over the years. He himself acknowledged that, as he matured, his ideas had changed. For instance he is capable, in retrospect, of condemning his own work in no uncertain terms. In the *True Principles* he writes: *I have perpetrated these enormities in the furniture I designed some years ago for Windsor Castle. At that time I had not the least idea of the principles I am now explaining.*

CHAPTER 2

The *True Principles* and their Application to St James' Church

Fig 1 — Courtesy of Reading Library

The Principles of Architecture

Pugin begins his book *The True Principles of Pointed or Christian Architecture*, by first stating that design has to be *necessary for convenience, construction or propriety*. Secondly, *all ornament should consist of enrichment of the essential construction of the building*. These are the two principles by which he says *you may be enabled to test architectural excellence*.

On reading his introduction, other words that come to mind, and which have been applied to Pugin's work, are firmness and delight; symmetry and economy. These in turn evoke the great principles of architecture: *firmitas, utilitas* and *venustas,* laid down in the first century BC, by the Roman architect, Vitruvius. Readers may have their own preferences on how best to translate these terms but the idea of *firmitas* or *solidity* is reflected in Pugin's commitment to *construction* whereas *utilitas* equates with his concept of *propriety* or *convenience,* which today we would call being 'fit for purpose'. V*enustas* (beauty) sits neatly with Pugin's definition of *ornament.*

It is worth reproducing a few more quotes from Pugin's *True Principles.* They serve to give us a flavour of his approach to the practical work of designing a building. At one point he writes: *In pure architecture the smallest detail should have meaning or serve a purpose.* Elsewhere he makes the contentious statement, especially with regard to St James': *it is in pointed architecture alone that these principles have been carried out.*

I shall also consider *ornament* with reference to the three principles, looking at the techniques of construction, be they in stone, metal or timber.

In *The True Principles* Pugin treated each element of church design in order, starting with the columns and buttresses. I shall follow that same order here.

COLUMNS AND BUTTRESSES

Principle: *It is evident that for strength and beauty, breaks or projections are necessary.*

Even in such a small church as St James', Pugin adheres to this principle. He breaks the lines of the long north and south walls by a regular series of five bays consisting of alternating windows and simple buttresses. The vertical line is compensated for by the use of equally regular horizontal string-courses. These serve not only as ornamentation but follow the principle of *utility*, by virtue of their weathering function. The bottom course, or plinth, is splayed, or bevelled, to take the water run-off away from the base. The whole achieves an effect appropriate to the scale of the building or, as Pugin would argue, follows the principle of *propriety*. It is worth commenting that in his only other Norman Romanesque church, at Gorey in Ireland, the base does not have this feature; the wall extends down to ground level.

Note the use of 'clamped' or 'clasping' buttresses at the corners of the west end (Fig 2). The earliest drawing we have (Fig 1) does not seem to show a clamped buttress at the east end. Subsequent alterations have made it difficult to establish what the eastern buttresses were like. However the existing eastern corner buttresses are much wider than those either at the west end or along the walls. Other contemporary sketches indicate this may have been the case when the church was first built.

Photographs of the original frontage clearly show this type of buttress at the west end, along with the string courses and splays mentioned above. There is another view of St James' in Reading Library, again attributed to W Fletcher, from Kennet Mouth looking across at the newly completed Great Western railway embankment. This is a very rough sketch but, from what can be made out, it supports the theory that the buttresses at the east end match those at the west in style but are in fact larger in width and depth.

If next we turn to examine the ashlar dressings of the buttresses in figure 2, we note the use of irregularly sized limestone corner stones or quoins. Pugin argues that if these are the same size *the eye is carried from the line of the jamb to them*. The same maxim is applies to window or door jambs.

He claims that a regular pattern to the quoins has the unfortunate effect of drawing the viewer's attention away to the peripheral parts of the structure, in other words outwards. So here, for example, the eye would be drawn towards the quoins and the buttresses and away from the intended foci of the building.

Pugin further states that small sized stonework not only makes construction stronger but also maintains the proportions, which would be destroyed by larger masonry elements. In addition he claims that stones in ancient buildings were not only small but *also very irregular in size so that the jointing might not appear a regular feature and by its lines interfere with those of the building.*

Fig 1 Photograph courtesy of St James' Church

The West Front

So what is the focus of attention, what was Pugin asking the building to do and what reaction does he expect from the viewer? He is explicit in his writings that a church exists for the glory of God and to connect man with his Creator.

Pugin wrote that *the history of architecture is the history of the world.* All forms of architecture may be *perfect expressions* but they are perfect expressions of *imperfect systems.* Only true Christian worship of the one true Christian God is the *perfect system,* and pointed architecture is the culmination of that development, *the crowning result,* of all previous Christian forms of architecture. He attacks the architectural

124

changes at the Reformation in the 16th century as not a *matter of mere taste, but a change of soul.*

Here lies a clue, in his own writings, as to Pugin's thoughts about designing in a non-pointed style. He claims that *previous to this period architecture had always been a correct type of the various systems.* Tie this in with his evolutionary view of Christian architecture and we can see how he could justify the use of the Norman Romanesque style. It should be remembered that Pugin spent much of his early life staying with relatives in Northern France and made many visits to the great churches of Normandy. He was as well versed in the development of architecture in Northern Europe in the Middle Ages as anyone could be; a claim he certainly made for himself.

I leave the readers to come their own conclusion about the focus of attention at the west end of St. James'. To me, however, there are two: the entrance to a holy place and the surmounting bellcote, which originally supported a cross.

The eye is drawn inwards and upwards. Our immediate focus is the great door, inviting the viewer into the home of the *sacred mysteries.* The idea of the pointed arch is to facilitate and reflect an ever upward or heavenly movement. The fact that Pugin achieves this effect with the use of rounded arches displays his architectural skills. The sketch in Marianna Frederica Cowlsade's book fully confirms this conclusion. The effect is completed by the eye being drawn first to the bell-cote and finally to the cross. It is important to note that there is a matching cross surmounting the east gable.

Whether Mangan, the architect of the 1926 alterations, respected or contradicted Pugin's design is a matter of opinion. Bringing the lower half of the west gable forward certainly gave the church greater depth and so more room. But was this at the cost of sacrificing propriety, convenience, construction, and so beauty, to utility? Would Pugin have considered the design as inconsistent, and thus undesirable?

Pugin's heading, and mine, to this section mentions 'columns.' I shall look at columns and pillars later when considering the west door in detail.

PINNACLES

Principle*: Pinnacles should be regarded as answering a double intention, both mystical and natural.*

Pugin says that pinnacles are not ornamental excrescences. They are not there merely for picturesque effect, but they serve two purposes, mystical and natural. St James' does not possess pinnacles but it does have a bellcote which to some extent served the same mystical intention. As we have just seen, the use of the cross surmounting the east gable and the bellcote at the west end, as in the drawing, serves both purposes: *Their mystical intention, like other vertical lines in Christian architecture, is an emblem of the Resurrection,* and draws the viewer's gaze ever upwards. Unfortunately the bellcote cross was later removed. Compare the two pictures below.

The bellcote draws the eye upwards, pointing like a finger to heaven. It is symbolic but also practical in that it houses the bell.

For Pugin the bell is not a mere embellishment. It may be an ornament but only in so far as it fulfils its liturgical purpose. It is the means by which *the faithful may be called to their devotions.* As such it is placed in an appropriate tower or belfry. In the case of St James', the bellcote, as we have seen, is highly visible and was originally crowned with a stone cross. Because of its height it is difficult to appreciate the care taken in its construction. Closer examination shows that the detail of the bellcote and its mouldings are consistent with every aspect of Pugin's *Principles.*

It is worthwhile recalling that under the 1791 Catholic Relief Act, bells were explicitly forbidden to Catholic Chapels. They were only allowed following the 1829 Catholic Emancipation Act. Their symbolism was therefore understood by Catholics and non-Catholics alike and enshrined in the law of the land. It is worth noting that the report in *The Tablet* explicitly mentions this important feature.

THE ROOF

PITCH   Principle: *The pitch of the roof: the most beautiful pitch of a roof or gable-end is an inclination sufficiently steep to throw off snow without giving the covering too perpendicular a strain; it is formed by two sides of an equilateral triangle. If this form is departed from, the gable appears either painfully acute or too widely spread. All really beautiful forms of architecture are based on the sound principles of utility. The practical aspect is that the correct pitch ensures the wind pressure bears down on the roof covering and not allowing the wind to blow under it so lifting it up.*

Modern view

Photograph by Henry Taunt, 1880s

Pugin stated that if that formula is departed from the *gable appears either painfully acute or too widely spread*. Pugin may have been strict in voicing his principles but at times principles may throw up apparent contradictions. Does the roof of St James' follow the equilateral principle and what is its impact?

Questions need to be asked as to whether he had formulated this principle by 1837 and when did he in fact apply it. I have compared the façades of several early designs such as St Michael's, Gorey, and St Peter's College, Wexford, and we see similar pitches in both these cases. Indeed if we look at Cheadle, his masterpiece, it would appear that he maintains a flexible attitude to pitch. Whatever Pugin's thinking in stating his principle about the angle of the pitch, he repeatedly commented on the necessity to take the local climatic conditions into account. He comments in the *Principles…* that: *our northern climate requires an acute pitch of roof to prevent the accumulation of snow and to resist weather.*

Sprocketed roof at St James'

At St James', the pitch accommodates the eaves by splaying slightly outwards, a technique known as a sprocketed roof. This method is employed when using roof beams and associated eaves that need to project well over the walls of the structure. It is noticeable that in the Fletcher-Wheble drawing this refinement is not present. A practical advantage of a sprocketed roof is that it allows greater depth to the eaves and so aids the anti-weathering process as rain-water is taken away from the walls. It also serves the important purpose of slowing down the flow of water.

GABLES

The gable copings and kneelers are of especial interest. In the Fletcher-Wheble drawing the kneeler and the corbel of the northwest gable appear to be missing, whereas they are present on the eastern gable. In fact on the actual building they are very prominent and this is a feature of Pugin's early designs. The coping stones of the gable are rounded and project out horizontally, at the base of the gable, quite significantly. In this way they become integrated with the kneeler, resting on the shaped corbel some way below. They share these features with St Michael's, Co. Wexford. As Brian Andrews comments in his work about Gorey, Pugin's *mature treatment of this detail had flat-topped coping stones, often terminating in a gablet, with the corbel generally directly below the kneeler.*

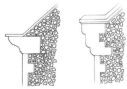

Evolution of the kneeler. To the left a standard kneeler from the 18th century: to the right Pugin's early kneeler design as found at St James' (© JR Mullaney)

THE EAST END

The eastern gable is likewise remarkable. The internal rounded chancel apse is reflected on the outside by the construction of the semi-conical roof which, before the addition of the ambulatory in the 1960s, gave the church its unique compact appearance. The use of dressed stone rather than flint for part of east end is also

128

worth noting. As I said before, it would appear that the stone was only used down to the level of the eaves of the conical roof, although on the Fletcher-Wheble drawing it would appear the intention was that it should be used for the whole gable. It is worth observing that Pugin only employed the use of a rounded apse in his Romanesque designs, namely in St James', St Michael's, and in the crypt of St Chad's.

MOULDINGS

Principle: *Mouldings are the enrichment of splays, doorways, windows, arches, piers, bases and string-courses, of weatherings and copings, and they are introduced solely on the principle of decorating the useful.*

Mouldings, as well as adding to the *enrichment* of a building, are also part of the *essential construction.* Splays allow extra light in the case of windows and at the base of buildings they protect and shed water off plinths. Mouldings, when used, should therefore reinforce these purposes. For the sake of beauty Pugin demanded that their effect on shadows must be considered. Gradations of light avoid monotony and enhance the beauty of the building.

The purpose of the essential construction of doorways is to allow access and egress. They should be the right width for their purpose and any ornament should contribute practically and aesthetically to this end. So, in the case of a door jamb, the mouldings should not project, as this would counteract the purpose of a splayed jamb: to increase width of access.

However the opposite is true for the outside of windows. There needs to be a hood mould projecting immediately above the arch to *receive water running down the wall.* The mould is not a mere ornament but part of the *essential construction* of directing water run-off. Note that the mouldings around the arch of the west door at St. James' are more divided than around the jamb. Why? This follows the same principle as found in nature *where the solid trunk spreads and divides as it rises upwards* – recalling the Vitruvian principle of *venustas.* Likewise where the arch joins the jambs, at the springing, continuity is best achieved through the use of foliated and moulded projections. Where the same moulding is used, from jamb through to arch, then there is no need for caps (small capitals).

The mouldings are an integral part of the design. As Pugin says in his *Apology* it is essential that *ornament is originated by the* edifice and not superimposed, or *adapted* as he puts it, onto the design. So, if we examine the west front, we see that the moulding over the door and windows carries on, becoming a string-course and so not only pleases the eye, but also serves a practical function. As noted above, this technique also serves to draw the eye back to the centre of the building. More specifically, at ground level the onlooker's gaze is led to the west door and so upwards.

Should the eye linger on the projections of the buttresses, then it is directed not inwards but upwards, to the coping which meets with another string-course moulding. Thus it completes the process of returning the focus of attention back to the centre of the building, to the rounded arch, up towards the oculus and so to the bellcote and, originally, the cross. Just in case the eye wanders again, the bevelled coping at the top of the buttresses points to the corbels and kneelers which in turn draw the eye to the gable coping and so back to the bellcote.

Pugin emphasises the need for splayed or bevelled coping, be it at the base of the building or surmounting any projection, such as we see on the top of the buttresses at St James'. If this were not so *they would become lodgments for water*, he says. At St James' each buttress has a bevelled or splayed top. It is worth noting the repeated use of scalloped decoration, a feature, almost an *idée fixe,* throughout the Church. We must assume this is a conscious reference to the symbolic significance of the scallop shell and its association with St James of Compostela. The ancient Abbey of Reading and the new Church share this religious connection, both being dedicated to St James.

Little remains of the north or south sides of Pugin's original design. We can, however, see that his use of mouldings over the windows, and their associated string-courses, projecting along the length of the building, serve a twofold function. There is once again their practical weathering purpose but aesthetically they serve to accentuate the unity of the building. Pugin retains a balance between the vertical and perpendicular and this is achieved through his careful placing of the splayed, round-arched windows and buttresses linked by the string-courses, which, as we saw above, are a continuation of the hood-moulds.

THE MOULDINGS AND THE WEST DOOR

Before looking more closely at the mouldings, it is worth noting how the plinths are splayed or bevelled to take water away from the base of the building. This technique also draws the eye upwards and in the case of the doorway, into the church. It is quite remarkable how closely the door mouldings follow those in *The True Principles*.

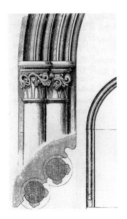

From *True Principles*   The west door of St James'

Pugin argues that a doorway needs not only to be large and properly proportioned but its *ornament* must complement its structural purpose. If we examine the proportions of the doorway at St. James', we see that the splay doubles the apparent size of the actual door opening. The width, Pugin argues, must not be increased or reduced by the depth of the mouldings. If too shallow they will produce an appearance of weakness in the jamb, if they project too far then the opening is narrowed and becomes inconvenient.

Note the use, at St James, of typical Norman Romanesque zigzag mouldings. It is interesting to see the scalloping theme being repeated on the outside 'order.' The 'caps' are likewise fluted or scalloped. This is a theme repeated throughout both the interior and exterior of the Church and is even found on the guttering and rain pipes. Mangan copied this in his 1926 alterations.

When looking at the buttresses we saw how Pugin insisted that the outline of the quoin stones must not interfere with the impact of the mouldings. Once again this is achieved by the use of irregular projections of the stones around the door jamb. The same is true for the windows above.

In the *Principles* Pugin lays great stress on the bonds and joints. In his drawings, below, Pugin demonstrates how large blocks of stone detract from the overall effect of a window or a door. The *eye*, he says, *owing to the regularity of these projections, is carried from the line of the jamb to them.* In the pictures below Pugin illustrates how, in the case of the top two, the eye is drawn towards the buttresses in the right hand picture, whilst the focal point is the window in the left hand drawing. In the case of the lower two drawings, in the left hand window the regular jamb stones lead the eye to the periphery of the window whilst in the right hand picture the irregular and smaller jambs accentuate the window itself.

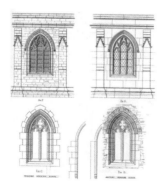

From *True Principles...*

If we look at St James', we see that the stones are of irregular size and projection. This is true both for the upper windows and the door. Far from the eye being drawn outwards and so concentrating on them, the stones become barely noticeable.

The string-courses not only satisfy the eye by continuing the line of the caps at the top of the column and base of the arch, but also serve the practical purpose of throwing the water off the wall and down to the next bevel, which in this case is the base of the building.

Pugin states that *all mouldings should be designed on the principle of light, shadow and half tint,* so *as to produce pleasing gradations of light and shadow.* This aesthetic

132

feature corresponds to the practical function of splays. In other words the projections caused by mouldings must follow the line of the splay and not protrude so as to interfere with access. At the same time the very same projections cause a play of light and shadow which enhances the beauty of the building. As Pugin puts it, a *projecting mould in such a situation would be a useless excrescence*. The importance of light leads us to Pugin's next topic for consideration, that of windows.

THE WINDOWS

Principle: *It will be readily seen that without a splay a considerable portion of light would be excluded, and that this form of jamb is necessary to the use and intention of a window.*

Splayed and un-splayed windows. From *True Principles*
(The shaded areas depict the masonry, with the dotted lines showing the line of the light.)

The window openings at St James follow this principle without equivocation. The overall result is a feeling of airiness. Wherever one sits in the nave at least two full windows and their light are visible.

Splayed window St James' Church   *Photograph C Widdows*

The above photo illustrates the validity of Pugin's claim about dispersing light. He is copying a style and technique frequently used in the Middle Ages. At a time when glass was are very expensive. Small apertures served a double purpose. They were useful in maintaining an even temperature. They lessened heat loss in winter and heat gain in summer.

133

Anyone visiting a church in Southern Europe will know how refreshing it is to step inside when the temperature is soaring outside. Should you visit the same church in winter, maybe with snow on the surrounding hills, then the interior, warmed even just by candles, retains its heat owing to the thickness of the walls and narrowness of its windows. Of course in Medieval Europe, as the structures became lighter, as glass became relatively less expensive and as windows became larger, this became less true. But in small, not very wealthy country churches, little changed.

Norman windows in a South Oxfordshire church

THE GLASS

There are several examples of the original stained glass in the Church. The glass that fills the oculus in the West gable is unfortunately obscured by the organ. A fraction can be spotted at various angles within the church.

For some time there has been discussion as to whether the existing apse windows are in fact the originals. There were claims that they had been removed for the duration of the Second World War and later replaced by different windows.

The internal evidence of the content of the windows, such as the use of the coats of arms of the various benefactors and the founder of the Church, would certainly indicate that they are indeed those originally installed. We know, for certain, that the brasses on the font were placed there at the time of the opening of the Church. An examination of these shows that the same heraldic devices are used on the brasses and in the windows. This gives us a very strong indication that they were designed at the same time. The possibility that the windows were made afterwards and merely copied these designs is lessened if we look at a contemporary report in the *Tablet* which gives a detailed description of them at the time of the Consecration of the Church in August 1840: *But in the whole and in the detail, the building is another trophy to the fame of the immortal architect. Immediately on passing the finely-*

wrought doors, the spectator's eye is carried to the eastern end, where, under the noble arch of the sanctuary, stands the altar, presenting at the first view a blaze of glory. Directly over it are three painted windows, of which the softened brilliancy of colouring produces the effect of clustered precious stones.

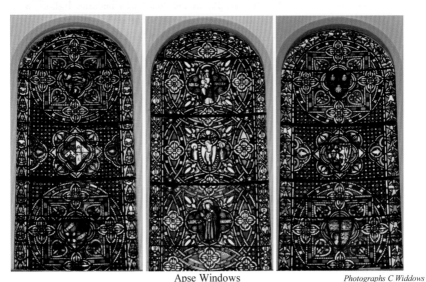

Apse Windows   *Photographs C Widdows*

It would be difficult to better the description: *the softened brilliancy of colouring produces the effect of clustered precious stones.* Moreover we have the evidence of photographs taken in the 19th or very early 20th century of the interior of the church. Although in black and white, the design of the windows and their patterns match those of the existing windows. It is quite possible that these were later additions or copies but the balance of probability rests with the conclusion that these are the original windows.

19th or early 20th Century interior view of St James'

THE METALWORK

Pugin next examines what he calls *consideration of works in metal.* He supplies his reader with copious examples and, as ever, lays down strict guidelines or 'principles' suiting, as he puts it, *the design to the material and decorating construction.* In other words his same initial three principles are to be applied as much to ironwork as to any other part of the building.

Locks, hinges, bolts, nails etc. should not be hidden. Their function is clear and they should be converted into things of beauty. Pugin points out that a modern hinge, shown at top right in the above plate, though hidden, is also weak. The same applies to locks and keys.

Leaves and crockets are not to *be carved or modelled and then cast.* Rather they should be *cut out of thin metal plate and twisted up with pliers and the lines of stems either engraved or soldered on.... Large tracery* should be *either formed of round iron, like a stem twisted into intersections, or of flat iron bars of different thicknesses riveted together, and the edges chamfered by filing.*

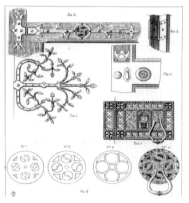

From *True Principles ...*

Pugin acknowledges that cast iron is valuable for mechanical purposes but should never be used for ornamentation. This is especially true when cast iron is used in conjunction with stone. For example a stone pillar is bulky whilst a cast iron pillar is relatively slight. The result is a miss-match between the dimensions of the two materials. Consequently, because of its inherent volume, a *great inconsistency* in the relationship between the materials occurs. However, if the tracery is reduced in size to match the strength of the material, then it looks *painfully thin, devoid of shadow and out of proportion to the openings in which they are fixed.* Another fault, as Pugin saw it, of cast iron, is the *repetition, subversive of variety and imagination.*

136

THE METAL WORK IN ST JAMES' CHURCH

There have been two periods of major changes to the Church. Consequently it is necessary to distinguish which features belong to each era.

The front doors appear to be original, dating back to the Pugin frontage. Notice the strength of the ironwork (Fig 1). This is designed, along with its associated inset hinge (Fig 2), as one of a pair to support a heavy studded door (Fig 3), yet the metal work is neither rough nor thick. Once again *The Tablet* gives us our first record and description when the author writes: *Immediately on passing the finely-wrought doors....* This evidence is rather tenuous. Notice that the author doesn't specifically mention metal work. However the use of the word 'wrought' most probably refers to the ironwork as well as to the doors themselves. The interior doors and ironwork we see today are not the originals, and date from the Mangan alterations.

As Pugin says, the flat iron is worked, not pre-moulded, into shape. *The wrought iron is then chamfered by filing giving it a pleasing rounded delicacy that belies its strength and function.* Notice, in Fig 2, the method employed to reverse the angle of the hinge, so that this is covered when the door is closed, thereby ensuring greater security. Pugin would argue that this conforms with all three of his main principles.

 Fig 1

Photographs C Widdows

 Fig 2

 Fig 3

Figure 3 clearly shows the internal doors, dating from the 1926 extension, leading from the narthex to the nave.

Contrast the Pugin hinges in figures 1, 2 and 3 with those on the interior doors designed by the architect Wilfred Mangan. (Figs 4 and 5)

Fig 4

Photograph C Widdows

Fig 5

These are much coarser, lacking the delicacy and ornamentation of the previous ironwork. It is interesting to note that the same ironwork is also used for the outside door hinges leading to the 'new' 1926 south aisle. (Fig 6)

Fig 6

Fig 7 *Photographs C Widdows*

The Sacristy Door

We now come across a conundrum: namely the existing door leading from the South aisle or Lady Chapel into the corridor to the Sacristy or vestry. Is it the original door that led from the Church into the original Sacristy?

The large metal work hinges (Fig. 7) look genuine and their quality is certainly superior to those we have just seen. Likewise the handle (Fig 8) is well worked and fulfils all Pugin's criteria of propriety and ornamentation. On the reverse side of the door we also see some high quality workmanship both in the woodwork and metal work (Fig 9). Notice that the wood planks on the outside are perpendicular whereas those on the insides they are set diagonally.

Photograph C Widdows

The question is whether this door was the original which led from the nave into the original sacristy.

 Fig 8  Fig 9

Photograph C Widdows

It contrasts with the one leading from the Sacristy to the Sanctuary which was clearly added at a much later date, possible in the 1926 restoration or even in the 1960s.

Fig 10   *Photograph C Widdows*

Figure 10 shows one of the pair of Baldwin hinges on the door between the sanctuary and the sacristy. The Baldwin company was established in the late 18th century. It was a family firm based at Stourport. (Stanley Baldwin, the politician and Prime Minister was descended from the founder.) Having moved to Stourport from Shrewsbury, the firm was certainly operating at the time Pugin designed St James' Church. One query is whether the connection with Shrewsbury meant that they were known to the Talbot family and so to James Wheble, or even to Pugin.

I am very doubtful that these Baldwin marked hinges were taken from any of the original doors. Their style and quality just do not match with the other metal work we see around the church. However the firm was still in business, specialising in hinges, in the 1920s, so it is possible that the hinges were supplied then, during the Mangan alterations

THE MAIN WEST DOOR LOCK AND KEY

Photographs C Widdows

The main West door lock and key appear to date from the original Pugin church. The lock mechanism is bolted to the door and, as Pugin writes in the *Principles, ... So far from being unsightly* (they) *are beautiful studs and busy enrichments.* However, possibly in keeping with the greater simplicity of the Norman style, the lock itself is not decorated. The studs are interesting. Close examination of the bottom right hand stud, when the photograph is enlarged, appears to show what may be Pugin's 'martlet' or stylised bird. This is however very speculative. Pugin had just begun using this now famous heraldic device in his new house, St Marie's Grange, Salisbury, in the late 1830s. Certainly all the studs show their 170 or so years' wear and details are difficult to discern. Neither the key nor the lock is as ornate as those Pugin portrays in his various books of designs. On the other hand he may have considered this more in keeping with the Norman style of architecture.

THE FONT

We saw how the font came to be discovered, how it was originally placed at the entrance to the nave and the significance of the brass plates on two of its sides. In his letter of August 1840 to Father Ringrose, Pugin is far from complimentary about the way the font has been treated. He complains that, *the font requires lining with lead and a cover with a lock. The brass plates on the font are exceedingly ill done the purport of the inscription is good but the Letters & heraldry are in the worst possible taste.*

Photograph C Widdows

The font was indeed subsequently lined and a cover with iron hinges and lock claspings fixed to it. It appears to have undergone several changes over the years. The ironwork however is Puginesque in style and probably dates to the 1840s. The brasses give the origin of the font and details about the opening of the church. The devices on the coats of arms are reproduced in the apse windows.

The Font brasses

Photographs C Widdows

141

THE WOODWORK

Principle: *The strength of woodwork is attained by bracing the various pieces together on geometrical principles. The construction of these, so far from being concealed, is turned into ornament.*

In his second lecture, Pugin begins by looking at decoration *with regard to constructions in wood*. As ever, he illustrates his words with examples and contrasting the ideal *ancient roofs with the framing made ornamental* against *the modern roof with framing concealed*.

Pugin was totally opposed to covering the joists with plaster, although he himself did just that on at least one occasion. However, overall he retained this principle. Let us read his own words: *the strength of wood-work is attained by bracing the various pieces together on geometrical principles... The principal tie-beams, rafters, purloins* (sic*), and braces, which in modern edifices are hidden at a vast expense by a flat plaster ceiling, are here rendered very ornamental features, and this essential portion of a building becomes its greatest beauty.*

From the *Principles...*

Ornamentation itself serves a purpose, or *appropriate meaning* as he expresses it. The carvings and paintings carry a mystical message such as the sight of angels *hovering over* the *congregated faithful*. Carving of angels and saints, together with holy scriptural emblems, enriched with paintings of the firmament, contribute to the *mystical meaning* of a church.

ST JAMES' ROOF

The roof structure of St. James' remains unaltered from the time of Pugin. As such it has great architectural and historical significance, not just for St James' but also for Reading. Moreover it is indeed, arguably, the church's most attractive feature, *its greatest beauty*, as Pugin himself called it.

As much of the terminology may be unfamiliar to readers two drawings of St James' roof structure are shown below. Figure 1 shows the basic 'queen strut' design as used in the church. The drawing shows what is called a 'principal'. Principals are the structures which are spaced along the length of the roof, marking the main bay divisions.

Fig. 1

The 'queen strut' design of St. James' roof

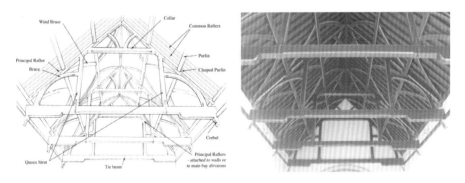

Fig 2 The labelled full roof structure of St James' Church

Photograph and drawings © JRMullaney

As can be seen from figure 2 this type of structure takes its name from the 'queen struts': the two upright posts attached to the piece of wood which stretches across the width of the building, the tie beam. The remaining elements of the structure serve as reinforcements both to the roof itself and to its supporting beams.

Partly because the roof structure in its entirety is the only remaining original piece of Pugin's design, it is also one of the most interesting. The eye is attracted by those geometric patterns which we have seen described by Pugin.

There is neither over-embellishment nor redundant usage of braces, tie beams or principals. The main tie beams consist of two joists fastened together, with an additional shorter third support resting on the corbels. This creates extra tensile strength, such as afforded by a leaf spring.

Fig 3   Leaf or carriage spring

It is of passing interest to note that the leaf spring is one of the oldest forms of spring and was used in the Middle Ages. Pugin, with his appreciation of all things medieval, was most probably aware of this. Reinforcement and solidity are sustained by using iron clasps and bolts. The overall effect is to give the roof much greater flexibility and so resistance to wind and weather pressure.

Fig 4

The Pugin roof showing the Queen Strut design at St James' Church. *Photograph C Widdows*

Over the years the tie beams have been subjected to some changes. The major one was the introduction, towards the end of the 19th century, of electric lighting. The chandelier hangings, visible in an early 20th century postcard, look very like those fitted in other churches in Reading and supplied by the Reading Electrical Company. The marks of the fixings can still be discerned on the tie beams. There is also painting on much of the woodwork and the corbels. I have found no records to date to tell how much of this is original or touched up from the original.

Finally let us take a look at a photograph, taken from the choir loft at the end of the 19th or the beginning of the 20th century, showing many of the features we have discussed in this book. There are some changes from what members of the very first choir would have seen looking down the nave to the altar.

The electric light fittings were added towards the end of the 19th or the beginning of the 20th century. But notice the gaslights between the Stations of the Cross. Also note the memorial to François Longuet. We can see a large tombstone with some form of crest just in front of Longuet's small brass plaque. Was Pugin's suggestion for a more elaborate memorial followed? Did these altar rails feature in the original design or was there a rood screen? The splayed windows in the nave are certainly fulfilling Pugin's promise of airiness and light. The 1960s alterations to the apse have detracted from the original intended function of its three windows, which was to flood the altar and sanctuary with light. However the stained glass windows, as argued above, do appear to be those we see today.

St James' after the installation of electric light fittings.

Even for those who know St James' there is so much more to be observed and discovered. For those unfamiliar with the church, a visit will offer a fascinating insight into the life, past and present, of the building and its place in the community.

St James' is a space rich in architectural heritage not merely fulfilling the needs of its thriving modern congregation but ideal for engaging with the people of Reading and beyond: a building Pugin could be proud of, as truly suited for its purpose!

CONCLUSION

This tour of the Church and examination of its salient architectural features demonstrate how closely Pugin adhered to the *Principles* he wrote down three or four years later. Pugin's motto *En Avant*, 'onwards', was most apt. He was his own greatest critic and was more than ready to move forward in his thinking and design.

The features which remain of his very first church design at St James' do in fact follow those basic principles of architecture which Pugin espoused throughout his life. On occasions their interpretation varied, but the basics remained constant. For this reason St James' Church is an important architectural site and of special interest at a national level.

Pugin died young. And yet already, within his short lifetime, the term 'puginism' was widely used, not least in church design. His ideas came to dominate Victorian architectural theory and practice. Even those who rejected his adherence to strict neo-Gothic ideas were affected by them.

Pugin has been called a proto-functionalist, a precursor of Louis Henry Sullivan, the father of the modern skyscraper. Sullivan's dictum form *ever follows function,* recalls Pugin's own principle that the *smallest detail should have meaning and serve a purpose.* Pugin's house at Ramsgate, with his insistence on crafted detail, in many aspects foreshadowed William Morris, his Red House and the Arts and Crafts movement. Likewise the secular works of Waterhouse, such as the Natural History Museum, evoke the principles expounded by Pugin.

And yet there were aspects of his latter work, including his writings, which indicate that at the end of his life Pugin was thinking ahead to a post-Pugin era. What might have come next, we shall never know, but we can be sure that it would have followed his greatest architectural principle - *En Avant.*

POSTSCRIPT

The Abbey Ruins and the Forbury after 1841

James Wheble had acquired a reputation as a keen explorer of Reading's past. As we have seen, he had been extensively involved in, and indeed largely financed, the excavations of the Abbey Ruins. He had bought much of the site with the probable intention of making further archaeological excavations. On his death, however, it would appear that his son and heir, James Joseph, did not entertain similar ambitions.

In 1854 Reading Corporation bought the eastern section of the present Forbury gardens, including the hill, for £1200, of which James Joseph donated £400. A further £400 was raised by voluntary subscription with the balance of £400 coming from the Corporation. Here were created what became known as the Pleasure Gardens. They opened on Easter Day 1856. In 1859 a tunnel was made to link them with the main body of the Ruins. The western part of the Forbury continued to be used for fairs. After one such event, in 1854, the area was reported as being covered *with heaps of oyster shells, manure and other refuse.*

Colonel Blagrave sold this area to the town in 1860 for £6,010. It was decided that fairs should no longer be held there. However the character of this part of the Forbury differed from the eastern section where the emphasis remained on botanical display. The western side was for recreational use, with the area grassed over except for the outside walks and a gravelled parade ground. The two halves of the Forbury remained very different in character and were even separated by a wall. Some nine years later, in 1869, the Town bought twelve acres of King's Meadow for *recreational use,* thereby freeing the western part of the Forbury for other purposes. In 1873 it was incorporated into the Pleasure Gardens and the whole area became known as the Forbury Gardens. The Maiwand Lion was installed in December 1886.

As Taunt's view of 1875, taken from the tower of St Lawrence's, shows, the Forbury had by that date acquired the form we recognise today, with St James' Catholic Church, designed by one of England's greatest architects, forming a fitting backdrop to one of Reading's most beautiful and historically important areas.

Courtesy Reading Library

The Abbey Ruins and Reading Today

The Reading of today is a very different place to the one that gave sanctuary to those French Priests over two hundred years ago. And yet there are many similarities.

In the course of this book we have looked at the differences and disputes between religious and ethnic groups, both in the country at large and in the town itself. During much of the 19th century there was the suspicion and fear that Catholics wanted to exercise their own interpretation of the law, with a foreign cleric, the Pope, dictating terms to the British Parliament. There was a similar outcry in our own century when the Archbishop of Canterbury proposed that there might be room for sharia law within the English legal system.

Every Sunday, between 400 to 500 Catholics come, almost without notice, and certainly without adverse comment, to attend Mass at St James' in the Abbey Ruins. They come from a rich variety of national and ethnic backgrounds. Over forty languages are represented in the Congregation: a true microcosm of modern Reading.

Today Catholics are respected and valued members of our society. If this book carries any message then it is that history is able to teach us lessons for a harmonious future.

The fact that Reading still has the Abbey Ruins, the Forbury Gardens and Pugin's first church, is largely thanks to that once outlawed, feared and distrusted group, the Catholics of Reading.

Let us hope that in another 200 years time someone will be writing a similar story to the one we have told in this book and that it will be of even wider reconciliation between communities

APPENDICES

A.   The French Priest's Poem

The following poem was originally written in French 'Alexandrines'. I have translated it into English blank verse, in the style of the period. L.M.

A Letter to the English People and Especially the Inhabitants of Reading
By N. Leguay, a French Priest

In the name of exiled priests and other French émigrés.

O English people, so munificent
To us, whom wise and loving Providence
Has kept for great and noble destiny!
Receive this grain of incense from my hands
And deign to listen to my feeble words,
The faithful homage of a grateful heart.

For five years, exiled from our cursèd land,
We have been welcomed by your sheltering arms.
This isle has saved us from the raging storms
Which raged about us, threatening our lives.
Your eyes are ever open to our needs.
No father for his son had such a care.
Your hands, for both delight and usefulness,
Have placed us in this lovely, fertile plot,
Designed to dazzle us with all its charms,
A masterpiece of God's creative skill.

Here, in the splendour of her bright array,
Intoxicated by the radiance
Of fairest Nature, who would not be moved,
Who not admire her freshness and her charm?
Oh how I love these orchards and these woods,
These stately castles and these fruitful fields;
Green meadows flanked by newly planted trees
With gambolling sheep and sweetly bleating lambs
The proud and lofty heads of elm and fir
And, far away, the frowning mountain peaks;

These fertile meadows and abundant fields
In summer all ablaze with burgeoning wheat;
Whole families of plants in ordered rows,
The new-grown saplings in their nurseries.
And all the wingèd singers of the air
Whose harmonies and concerts give such joy.
In silence I admire this charming play
Its grace, its richness, its magnificence.
My eye with ardour and with eagerness
Devours anew the beauty that I see;
Each aspect of this tableau I applaud
To see it daily is a constant joy.
Between these flowery meadows and these slopes

The Thames, with her attendant twenty streams,
Makes stately progress through the fruitful vale.
She leaves regretfully her watered plain
And as she grows and widens, so her mouth
Will soon be filled with countless boats and ships,
Which bear the treasure of new industry
And prosperous commerce on her shining waves.

Within the valley's verdant banks I see
Reading, enriched by Nature with her gifts.
Reading, blest exile, whose delightful walls
Such cheerful, kind and gentle folk enclose.
Their faces candid and serene appear,
Reflecting goodness, mirrors of their souls.

Here nothing breaks the charm of sweet repose.
Peace, lovely peace, keeps trouble far away.
Though civil strife may wave its brands abroad,
With fiery serpents and with poisoned words,
This sheltering roof, these walls, this refuge sweet,
Give to the virtuous stranger tranquil rest.
His grateful, brimming eyes in Reading see
Such eager benefactors, brothers, friends,
Who understand his troubles, share his woe.
The people haste to welcome him with joy;
The exile's sleep is peaceful, deep and long.
He wakes untroubled now by fear and dread
And walks unhindered through this happy land,
Enjoying everywhere such gracious smiles,
Such civil looks, such kindly courtesy,
Surpassing expectation, soothing pain.

O virtuous, happy people, justly so,
What can we offer you in recompense
For all the generous favours that your hands
Give to so many exiles every day?
Indeed, we say, your faithful hearts reflect,
And mirror that of your most gracious king,
A prince magnanimous and good and kind,
Who knows his people, working for their joy,
A king whose wisdom and whose reign display
The wakened might and fame of Albion.

You live your days under this best of kings,
His throne your shelter and his laws your shade
The steadfast, open manner of his rule
Erects no barriers between land and king.
Sometimes in Reading he graciously appears;
No pomp, no circumstance, no lengthy train,
No sentries circle him to guard his life,
But virtue follows, guards and shelters him.
A prince whose faithful subjects love him well,
Can show himself to all at any time.
What should he fear and who would do him harm?
His people's love is his most trusty guard.
Their hearts, which shelter him from any ill,
Are mighty ramparts for his sacred life.
He sees his subjects clustering all around,
A father figure at his family's heart.
Nothing more touching can sweet virtue see;
The world itself stands awestruck at the sight.

Yet this recalls, alas, to my sad soul
How things once stood in my ungrateful land
Such sweet and tender bonds, by law upheld,
Once linked the Bourbons to the men of France.
How times have changed. I see, where e'er I look,
The crimes of guilty subjects 'gainst their king.
Our altars smashed to powder, throne destroyed,
Without them are renown and virtue fled.
But France's rival, who observes her crimes,
Respects, maintains, and keeps the ancient law,
Despising all who innovation seek,
Knowing the value of her governance.
Her laws her compass, guide and buttress are,
Her prince her glory and her monument,
Thus England earns the title, in our eyes:
Most generous, wisest nation in the world.

B.. Obituary of Anna Maria Smart

READING MERCURY 1809

SATURDAY, MAY 20

On Tuesday the 16th instant, in the 78th year of her age, died, Mrs. Anna Maria Smart, upwards of five and forty years one of the principal Proprietors of this Paper.

Many of our readers will expect, and all, we trust, will excuse our entering into some details in regard to a Woman so much, and so deservedly respected, and who certainly was an uncommon character. She was a native of this Town, where her father, William Carnan, then sole Proprietor of this Paper, died in 1837, in the flower of his age, leaving a Widow and family, and a most irreproachable character. The subject of this paragraph was married in 1732 to Christopher Smart, of Pembroke Hall, Cambridge, A.M. the well-known Author of some approved Poems on the Divine Attributes, for which he obtained Mr. Seaton's prize five times, that is, as often as he attempted to write for it.

Mrs. Smart enjoyed for many years a fine state of health, which every winter has been undermining; but her uncommon fortitude and clearness of intellect continued unimpaired to the last. She settled her books on the eve of her decease, and was attempting to rise when she expired. – Never was disinterestedness more complete, or benevolence warmer or more active than her's; and no private individual was ever more extensively useful. A Catholic in religion, a Christian in the true spirit of the Character, she never enquires the principles of any who solicited her help; all in distress were her Neighbours, her Kinsfolk and Country-people.—The great services she rendered to the French emigrants being so well known, It would perhaps be superfluous, were it not to observe, that to assist Foreigners conspicuously, requires

Fortitude no less than Benevolence; for whoever is serviceable in any distinguished manner to the natives of another country, will infallibly incur the censure, and excite the jealousy, of all the narrow-minded of their own. To conclude, the Benevolence which was with her, at once feeling and sentinient (sic), was far too innate to excite her own admiration, or seek that of others; an d can never be fully appreciated till that last Great Day, when all who like her shall have imitated the Heavenly Father, in causing their sun to shine upon the good and upon the bad; and raining upon the just and the unjust, will be received with the promised, everlasting welcome: "Come, ye blessed of my Father," &c. &c. --- Matt. 25. 34

C. Catalogue of Longuet's Books at the Chapel of the Resurrection.

Author's Note: This list is a verbatim transcription of a document held in the Westmister Archives, Poynter Box. Genitive apostrophes are missing in the original.

There are 88 vols. in the collection. The list, together with explanatory notes, may be found in St. James' Church Archives.

Catechism of Christian Doctrine
    in Latin Folio
Blyths Sermons   4 Vols
Archers Sermons 4 Vols
Do do Second series 3Vols
Appletons Discourses
Discourses on the Grounds of
   Christian Belief by ?J H
Butlers Discourses 3 Vols
Bossuet's Variations 2 Vols
Chaloners Meditations 2 Vols
Butlers Lives of the Saints 10 Vols
Conferences d'Angers 25 Vols new
Mannings Truths 2 Vols
Doctrine of the Catholic Church
translated into English from Bossuet
Hays Sincere Christian 2 Vols

Hays Devout Christian 2 Vols
Gobinets Instruction for Youth –
Reeve's Christian Church 3 Vols
P Bakers Works 4 Vols
Douay Bible 5 Vols
Sacraments Explained by JH
Ten Commandments Do by Do
Christian Directory by R Parsons
Mannocks Poor Mans Catechism
Pensées Evangéliques pour chaque jour
de l'année 2 vols
Pseaumes *(sic)* de David avec des
   Notes
Instructions de la Jeunesse par Gobinet
Latin Testament
Latin Theology 6 Vols
Webbes Plain Chant

D. Consecration of St James' Church at Reading, The *Tablet,* August 1840

On Wednesday the 5th of August, the new Church of St. James, erected on the site of the once magnificent abbey at Reading, was solemnly blessed, and divine service was performed there, agreeably to the wish and design of the late lamented founder, James Wheble, Esq. The family of the deceased gentleman had no sooner recovered from the first effects of the blow inflicted upon them by his sudden death, than all their endeavours were directed to the pious duty of fulfilling, as far as possible, his favourite project on the very day appointed by himself. The limited space of time, and the unlooked for intervention of many obstacles, threw no discouragement of an intention honourable alike to the departed and the living. The intention, therefore, was with the blessing of the Almighty, solemnly and religiously, though with strict privacy, fulfilled: those members of the clergy only being present whose attendance was requested on the occasion.

On the following Sunday, the sound of their own church bell, a new sound to the Catholic inhabitants of Reading, was hailed by them with mingled grief and gratitude, and assembled them all under the stately roof of the newly completed building. A fine and most remarkable piece of sculpture, excavated three years since from its interment of three centuries under the ruins of the abbey, is now placed as a baptismal font in the aisle of the new church. Two sides of this valued relic are still adorned with the rich tracery of its sculptured ornaments in perfect preservation; on the other two, despoiled of these by time and injury, inscriptions have been placed, the one relating to the font itself; the other recording analogous events which no Catholic heart can peruse without emotion. It runs thus (Capitals and punctuation as in the original):

The Great Abbey of Reading was commenced A.D. 1121, AND THE Conventual Church was finished A.D 1125, and consecrated by St. Thomas of Canterbury, A.D 1164. The foundation stone of St. James's Church was laid Dec. 14, 1837, and Divine Service was first performed therein on the Feast of the B.V. ad Nives, Aug 5, 1840.

Comments and moralisms have not been spared in certain classes on the temerity of recording, as past, events that are to come. But those who do not confound the anxious zeal of a good Christian, in a holy cause with the vain glory of mere human ambition, are inclined to regard this inscription, piously borne out as it has been, rather as prophetic than as presumptuous. The church of St. James, though as compared with many of those now gloriously rising through the kingdom, it may be considered small, is unquestionably a noble building; and from the art of its proportions conveys an impression of grandeur not explained by its size, and of beauty which it does not owe to richness of decoration, for the walls within are perhaps severely plain. But in the whole and in the detail, the building is another trophy to the fame of the immortal architect. Immediately on passing the finely-wrought doors, the spectators eye is carried to the eastern end, where, under the noble arch of the sanctuary, stands the altar, presenting at the first view a blaze of glory. Directly over it are three painted windows, of which the softened brilliancy of colouring produces the effect of clustered precious stones. The perfect detail of every portion of the tabernacle and altar forms a constant attraction of which the eye is never weary.

At the western end is the choir, adorned also with two windows of singular beauty, and at the remote end of the choir is placed a powerful and richly-toned organ. It is so placed as not to intercept the view of the centre window. Every external part of the edifice is in strict accordance with the spirit and style of the architecture of the age to which it refers; and whatever difference of opinion may be allowed of different styles, there can be none in the decision that no other style would have been appropriate to the sacred spot on which it stands. The gentleman appointed to be pastor over the Reading congregation is the Rev. John Ringrose, domestic chaplain and most esteemed friend of the late Mr Wheble.

E. Pugin's Letter to Father Ringrose 22nd August 1840

This letter, including punctuation and spellings, is reproduced as exactly as possible to the original.

Rev'd Dear Sir,
          As I had not the pleasure of meeting you yesterday at Reading I hasten by letter to communicate to you the result of my observation(s) (respecting) St James' church.

1. The reading desk I saw in the sanctuary is most offensive it destroys the whole character of the chancel and is perfectly disgraceful a proper Lectern with a houseling* *(sic)* cloth of silk embellished with a simple cross would not be expensive and yet in character the present thing is <u>detestable</u>

2. I cannot conceive how the altar came to be painted a beastly brown colour. It was not by my orders I desired it to be left *(stone or alone)* with certain *(mouldings) (gilt)* it destroys the whole effect of the altar this must altered immediately and (*the crossed out*) paint a stone colour with the base mouldings gilt.

3. The inscription on the brass plate on the floor is miserable. It is precisely what a protestant might have stuck up to commemorate a murder it does not posess (sic) a particle of Catholic spirit either in matter or appearance I would undertake for £5 to have a small brass of a priest engraved with suitable inscription in *artist* Letters. this would be quite in character the present square plate signifies nothing

4   the naked appearance of the chancel is quite distressing I entrust of you to ascertain if the present Mr Wheble will consent to carry out the original design for the sacristy which would not be attended by much expense and really the whole effect of the interior is ruined by <u>its present naked appearance.</u> Without colour it is impossible to produce any effect

5. the things that are required for the finishing of the chancel are as follows. A Dossel* behind the Altar. 2 curtains of plush or silk 2 elevation candlesticks. a lamp suspended from the boss. a proper Lectorium. a Missal properly bound. & a sacring bell.

6. There must be some plain fittings for the sacristy – these should have a proper character

7th. (sic) The font requires lining with lead and a cover with a lock. The brass plates on the font are exceedingly ill done the *purport* of the inscription is good but the Letters & heraldry are in the worst possible taste

8 the organ pipes require painting & Drapery

9 I furnished the late Mr Wheble with drawings for an entrance gateway & a stone cross to stand in cemetery. (sic) I hope these will be carried out

10. I *(missing due to wax seal tear – possibly* beg distinctly*)* to state that I am quite ready to supply all the necessary drawings and superintendence for the things that are required to complete the church without fee or reward as I agreed with the Late Mr Wheble all that I am *anxious* for is that The building be compleated *(sic)* a very small outlay will do all that is required & at present for want of these decorations the internal effect is miserable pray send this letter to Mr Wheble & let me know his intentions in this matter. I shall be at the Earl of Shrewsburys for some days. so a letter addressed to me at Alton will be sure to reach me.

I remain with great respect
Your dvt svt *(Your devoted servant?)*   + A Welby Pugin

- Housling – sacramental
- Dossel – a cloth hanging behind an altar

Note. Words in italics are unclear in the original text. Pugin's use of capital letters, spelling and punctuation is most idiosyncratic and I have tried to replicate these as accurately as possibly. I have used italics in brackets for my own comments or suggested text. The letter is postmarked Aug 22nd 1840 There is no date on the letter itself. According to the tablet article of August 1840 the Church was solemnly blessed on the Wed 5th August, the *Feast of the Vigin ad Nives.* This is corroborated in the Cowlsade ms.

F. St. James' Archive Group

In 2011 Canon John O'Shea called a meeting asking for anyone interested to join the group. Several people even from beyond the Parish came along and out of this a core group was formed to catalogue the archives in the possession of the Parish. Dr Val Fontana came from Portsmouth to advise on 'archiving.' Members of the Archive Group subsequently visited Portsmouth to view the Archives and enjoyed a tour of the Cathedral and lunch at a portside restaurant. It is thanks to the many hours of painstaking work that the archives are now catalogued and available for public consultation.

The members of the archiving group were: Mike McDonagh, Bill Murphy, Jim Black, Mike Keep, John Mullaney Maggie Burton and Carole Van de Velde. The group was extended to work on other aspects of the history of St James'. The additional members were Sarah Scanlon, Tony Corley, Anne Davies and Lindsay Mullaney.

BIBLIOGRAPHY and SOURCES

We are not listing the hundreds of individual documents which may be found in the archives mentioned. The most important of these are detailed in the text. The list includes details directing future researchers to areas where material may be sourced.

Primary Sources

Berkshire Records' Office, *Woodley Lodge, Whebles. Various maps.*
Census Returns 1841 & 1851, *Catalogues and microfilm,* Reading Library.
The Cowslade Manuscript. *Transcribed and digitalised by Lindsay Mullaney from Archbishop King's transcription in the Portsmouth Diocesan Archives,* St James' Archives.
Cowslade, Marianna, *Sketch Book 1833,* Reading Library.
Fletcher, William, *Reading, Past and Present 1838,* Reading Library.
Gillow, Joseph, *The Haydock Papers,* General Books, USA, 2010.
Leguay, N, *Epitre à la Nation Angloise, et particulièrement aux Habitants de la Ville de Reading: Excerpt from 'Pièces de poésie'* St James' Archives.
Scantlebury, Robert Elliott, *Baptismal Registers, Woodley Lodge,* St James' Archives.
Porstmouth Diocesan Archives: Reading boxes.
Pugin, Augustus Welby, *An Apology for the Revival of Christian Architecture.*
Pugin, Augustus Welby, *The True Principles of Pointed or Christian Architecture.*
Pugin, Augustus Welby, *Contrasts.*
Reading Mercury: Microfilm, Reading Library.
St James Church Archives. Documents and photographs.
The Tablet 1840.
Westminster Diocesan Archives: Reading boxes, Letters from Poynter, Griffiths, the Smarts, etc.

Secondary Sources

The bibliography and secondary sources relating to the general history of the period covered are too extensive to list here. We have therefore restricted the list to those works which have a direct and unique bearing on our researches.

Atterbury, Paul, and Wainright , Clive (eds), *A.W.N. Pugin: Master of Gothic Revival.* New Haven 1994.
Bellenger, Dominic Aidan, *French Exiled Clergy in the British Isles after 1789,* Downside Abbey, 1986.
Bellenger, Dominic Aidan, *The French Exiled Clergy in Reading,* South Western Catholic History No. 2, 1984.

Burton, K G, *The Early Newspaper Press in Berkshire*, Reading Library.
Darter, William, *Reminiscences of Reading by an Octogenarian*, Reading Library.
Devlin, Christopher, *Poor Kit Smart,* Reading Library.
Hill, Rosemary, *God's Architect, Pugin and the Building of Romantic Britain,* London, 2007.
Eppstein, John, *History of the Faith in an English Town*, Reading Library.
Fisher, Michael, *Pugin-Land,* M Fisher 2002.
Hadland, Tony, *Thames Valley Papists,* 2004
Harrison, Lucy, *A Vanished Berkshire Family*, The Berkshire Archaeological Journal, 1933.
Leys, M.D.R., *Catholics in England,* The Catholic Book Club, 1961.
Mullaney, John, *St. James' Catholic Church and School*, St James' Archives.
Plasse, F. X., *Le clergé français réfugié en Angleterre.*
Scantlebury, Robert Elliott, *The Catholic Registers of Reading,* St James' Archives.
Schofield, Nicholas and Skinner, Gerard, *The English Vicars Apostolic*, Family Publications, 2009.
Slade, Cecil, *The Town of Reading and its Abbey*, Local Heritage Books 2001
Stanford, Eric, *History of Castle Hill House*, Unpublished, Reading Library.

Online Resources

Apart from the many usual Internet resources, I found those listed below particularly useful.

British History Online: www.british-history.ac.uk
Internet Text Archive: www.archive.org/details/texts
Looking at Buildings, an Architectural Dictionary: www.lookingatbuildings.org.uk
Plasse, F. X., *Le clergé français réfugié en Angleterre:*
http://archive.org/details/a604568902plasuoft
The National Archives: www.nationalarchives.gov.uk
The Oxford Dictionary of National Biography: www.oxforddnb.com/search/
The Peerage: www.thepeerage.com

The Authors

John Mullaney

Born in Beaconsfield in 1943 John attended Our Lady of Sion, Kensington, St Benedict's School, Ealing and The Salesian College, Chertsey. While a member of the Servite Order he studied Philosophy and Theology at the Gregorian University, Rome. John also attended the Università per Stranieri di Perugia where he became interested in architecture. He produced work for the Council of Europe on Italian Medieval and early Renaissance buildings. Whilst living in Italy he taught from Middle School to University levels. In England he studied History and Italian at Reading University where he met his wife, Lindsay.

On completion of his PGCE he taught at Hugh Faringdon Catholic Secondary School in Reading. He went on to take a Masters in Education at Reading University, specialising in the History and Philosophy of Education.

In 1969 John and Lindsay set up Caversham Bookshop. During this time John was involved in producing two books about the history of Caversham and wrote the first booklet about the history of St James' Parish. He joined the editorial team of the Caversham Bridge ecumenical newspaper and was its first Catholic editor. In 2004 John retired, became a school governor and engaged in his passions for gardening and historical research.

Lindsay Mullaney

Lindsay (née Stainthorp) was born in Preston in 1949. She went to Lark Hill Convent School run by the FCJ order. She attended Reading University where she gained a First in French and Italian.

On completing her PGCE she was appointed Head of Languages at Hugh Faringdon Catholic Secondary School, Reading. She became an examiner for Ordinary Level GCE and for Advanced Level French, in addition to being local Consortium Secretary for French CSE. She gained a Masters in Applied Linguistics from Reading University in 1979.

On leaving teaching she joined John in Caversham Bookshop. Lindsay became renowned not only as 'that nice lady in the bookshop', but also for her annual quizzes which raised many thousands of pounds for charities. She also ran various literary competitions connected with the Caversham Festival, which she and John helped to found.

Since retiring Lindsay has become a Hospital Chaplaincy Volunteer, making weekly visits to the Royal Berkshire Hospital. She is also a member of a local choir, Parenthesis, as well as St James' Church choir. She loves looking after her grandchild and introducing him to the delights of gardening.

Other Contributors

John R Mullaney - Illustrations

John is the elder son of John and Lindsay. He attended The Oratory School, Woodcote and took a degree in Visual Arts and Literature at Staffordshire University.

John produces property portraits and artist's impressions for the property market. His work is used by architects, property developers, planning consultants and archaeological conservationists. His film-licensing work has also gained international acclaim having been published in conjunction with several film companies such as Lucasfilm and Twentieth Century Fox. He is a Fellow and Council Member of the Society of Architectural Illustration.

John is also a longtime volunteer and magazine editor for the Newman Holiday Trust, a charity which provides summer holidays for children with special needs.

He is also a keen musician and is guitarist & songwriter with his band *Last Picture Show*.

John lives with his wife and family in Reading.

www.thetopdraw.com   www.newmantrust.org   www.myspace.com/lastpictureshowuk

Chris Widdows - Photographs

Chris Widdows was born in Reading in 1944; he attended Reading School where he spent many happy hours ensconced in the School's darkroom avoiding the cold and wet of the rugby field. Now in retirement he spends as much, if not more, time sitting in front of his computer manipulating digital images. He likes to respond to requests from local societies to record their events in the form of slideshows or to provide images that can be used in local newspapers, books and magazine.

CWiddows@aol.com

And

Special thanks also to our son **James Mullaney** for his technical support and advice.

Scallop Shell Press

If you would like to find out more about Scallop Shell Press then visit our website where you will also find details of many of the documents referred to in the text.

www.Scallopshellpress.co.uk   or use our QR code

Email: Scallopshellpress@yahoo.co.uk

2012

Scallop Shell Press

Ever since the Middle Ages the scallop shell has been the symbol of those going on pilgrimage to the shrine of St James in Compostela, Spain.

Today the pilgrimage is even more popular than ever as people of all faiths, and none, seek a meaning for their journey through life.

The shell became a metaphor for the journey, the grooves representing the many ways of arriving at one's destination. At a practical level the shell was also useful for scooping up water to drink or food to eat.

Scallop Shell Press aims to publish works which, like the grooves of the shell, will offer the modern pilgrim stories of our shared humanity and help readers arrive at their own meaningful interpretations of life. We hope that our books will be shells within whose covers readers will find an intellectual and spiritual source of sustenance for their own personal pilgrimages.